Praise

"Prophetic prose for leade
sidering the cost of the jo   ___g your unnecessary baggage, and
risking in the right direction as a follower of Jesus is more critical than ever!
As a pastor successfully planting in the pandemic, Jordan Biel's experience
as faith-filled leader sets the backdrop for exploring leadership lessons from
Joseph, Gideon, and Jesus. Enjoy!"

—Dave Pafford
EMERGE Executive Director of Program & Development

"This book is a must-read for every young leader endeavoring to make an eternal
difference. I've heard it said that joy is in the journey, not in the destination.
Jordan Biel does a masterful job not only of helping leaders navigate around the
pitfalls that could detour them from their destination, but also in immersing
us in the mindset necessary to find joy in every stage of the journey. If God has
given you a dream, this book will equip you to see it become a reality."

—Andy Lehman
Executive Director 415 Leaders

"Not only is Jordan a smart leader, he's a humble and Godly leader. PROCESS is
filled with wisdom, story, and pragmatic application to deepen your walk with
Abba, and to sharpen and root your leadership. Embrace the promise, embrace
the journey. This book is worth your time and energy."

—Christopher Beard
Peoples Church Cincinnati, Peoples Church Network, Author of *Remarkable*

"Whether you're a parent, teacher, businessperson, or pastor, the principles in
this book will help you become a better leader. Jordan weaves together seven
key threads that will strengthen your leadership development. One of those
threads, which you don't hear about often, is sonship. I love the way Jordan
uses our relationship with God the Father to put all other threads of leadership
into perspective. Jordan is a man who follows after God's heart, and that shines
through in The Process of a Leader."

—Paris Yanno
Director, *Father's Heart*

"Many young leaders fail to understand that one must go through a process of refining and development if they desire to see the fulfillment of the dream that God has put within their heart. Jordan Biel has explained that process with great insight and clarity. Every leader must understand this process so that they can develop into the mature son/daughter who can effectively receive the inheritance of that dream. When you understand this process, it will give you the strength to endure victoriously. Every leader would benefit tremendously from the reading of this insightful book."

—Richard Crisco
Senior Pastor Rochester First Assembly of God, Rochester, Michigan

"I've never met a pastor who got into ministry with the mindset they would eventually burnout and quit . . . yet so many do. But it doesn't have to be that way. Jordan does a great job giving every leader the "process" on how not just to make it to the end, but to enjoy the journey along the way. The Process of a Leader will help you establish guardrails to prevent you from drifting away from your God-given destiny."

—Kyle Hammond
Lead Pastor, Adventure Church, Columbus, Ohio

"Jordan is talented enough to do anything alone and succeed, but he refuses to live that way. He wants to bring everyone—believers, pastors, leaders, readers, etc.—along with him on his passionate journey of discovering Christ on a deep level. I have never met anyone so talented who refuses to be an egomaniac; he is genuinely more interested in your story than his own. God can do anything through such a man!"

— Pastor Matt Anderson
Assemblies of God journalist and host of *The Matt Cast* podcast

THE PROCESS OF A LEADER

Developing the heart of **Jesus** in your **leadership** and why it **matters** most

Jordan Biel

ARROWS&STONES

OTHER TITLES BY JORDAN BIEL

Truth & Love: Eternity and Freedom are in the Balance

The 7 Theory: Discover the Secrets to Hearing Music & Playing Music

The Hook: What Preachers Can Learn from Songwriters

Scripture quotations marked NIV are taken from the Holy Bible, New International Version®, NIV®. Copyright © 1973, 1978, 1984, 2011 by Biblica, Inc.™ Used by permission of Zondervan. All rights reserved worldwide. www.zondervan.com. The "NIV" and "New International Version" are trademarks registered in the United States Patent and Trademark Office by Biblica, Inc.™ | Scripture quotations marked NLT are taken from the Holy Bible, New Living Translation, copyright © 1996, 2004, 2015 by Tyndale House Foundation. Used by permission of Tyndale House Publishers, Inc., Carol Stream, Illinois 60188. All rights reserved. | Scripture quotations marked ESV are from The ESV® Bible (The Holy Bible, English Standard Version®), copyright © 2001 by Crossway, a publishing ministry of Good News Publishers. Used by permission. All rights reserved. | Scripture quotations marked HCSB are taken from the Holman Christian Standard Bible®, Used by Permission HCSB ©1999,2000,2002,2003,2009 Holman Bible Publishers. Holman Christian Standard Bible®, Holman CSB®, and HCSB® are federally registered trademarks of Holman Bible Publishers.

For foreign and subsidiary rights, contact the author.

Cover design by: Sonny Carder

ISBN: 978-1-954089-95-2   1 2 3 4 5 6 7 8 9 10

Printed in the United States of America

Dedication

This book is dedicated to my beautiful wife, Danielle. Danielle, you've taught me what it means to follow Jesus, to love people well—no matter what their background is or what questions they have. You allowed me to be gone many, many times to minister and follow my music dreams early in our marriage. You have sacrificed so much for the kingdom! You've shown me such incredible kindness. You were my best friend when I was fourteen, and you still are. You're still the love of my life, and I am so grateful that I get to follow Jesus with you and that we spend every day together! You are stunningly beautiful, inside and out!

Contents

FOREWORD

This book communicates people over products. As a pastor, planter, and passionate musician, Pastor Jordan Biel knows this in his soul. Carved out of his own experience and life lessons, this book explores what Jordan knows—that all too often, leaders sacrifice the most meaningful for the somewhat important. With a little perspective, leaders can find the compass pointing them to a more permanent purpose. In life, some things are more important than others. When you understand what's most important, your calling and your calendar find clarity.

Throughout this book, Jordan highlights the importance of the premise, the passion, and the promise. Leadership is often helping organizations—helping people—cope with change. The best leaders learn to smile and love through the pain. This is an ability that you can develop, like a Joshua, Gideon, or Jesus. Human passion, pain, and promise always have purpose.

Ideas, enhancements, improvements, developments, inspirations, and initiatives are important, but they are not what's most important. Suffering the small stuff is what it takes to create the big picture.

Tolkien once reminded us that shortcuts make long delays. In order to keep yourself—and those you lead—on the path of health long-term, you cannot circumvent the process. You've got to have a practice of process that includes biblical and mutual accountability, coaches, and wonderful counselors. A true friend will not just accept you for who you are; they will hold you to a higher standard. Joshua had Caleb. Gideon has his 300. And Jesus had the Holy Spirit.

You can learn to be more inventive, more ingenious, and more imaginative than you ever thought possible if you'll trust the process.

—DAVE PAFFORD

Executive Director of Development at EMERGE

INTRODUCTION

I'm so glad you're reading this. Perhaps someone gave you this book. Maybe you decided on your own to read it. Either way, the fact that you're reading it tells me that you're called to be a leader in the kingdom of God. Whether you're a businessman who follows Christ, a missionary who's traveling the globe, or a teenager who just knows that you want your life to matter—whoever you are, I'm thrilled you're going to take this journey with me. I encourage you to read with an open heart.

I was that teenager who knew that he wanted to make a difference in the world for God. I knew at a young age that I wanted God to use my life in some way. I wanted to be a world changer. My dad used to grab my shoulders, look me in eyes before I'd head out the door for school, and say, "Son, you're going to be a world changer!" The crazy thing is I believed him! Someone believes in you; maybe they're the one who gave you this book. I know one thing: even if you don't think there are many *people* who believe in you, *God* does!

If you'll activate the grace gifts that God's already given you and walk in the truth of being His child, you'll discover the joy that life is meant to have! I believe every child of God is uniquely wired to impact others with their God-given talents, all for the purpose of displaying Father God's love. Yet so many who have great potential to influence others never begin to truly lead—or worse, they begin the journey of becoming a leader but give up. Many leaders start strong, then end their leadership journeys because of a sexual affair, a loss of direction, or even a tragedy. That happens because they didn't know the process of a leader.

This book is an attempt to prevent any of these stories from being your story. You don't have to be a statistic. You can be a success—a true success! You won't quit because you'll know *the process* of becoming a godly leader and, ultimately, what leadership is all about. You'll know that the person God is making you into is more important than anything else.

I ran cross country as a teenager. If I hadn't known that I was in a race, how long that race was, and the reward that lay at the finish line, I would've easily been tempted to quit. If I hadn't been warned about the cramps and taught how to pace myself, I wouldn't have finished. If I had been told, "This is going to be easy! You'll love it. Piece of cake!" I would've given up after one mile—or less! Instead, I remember my coach telling me, "Jordan, this is going to hurt at times. You'll get cramps in your side; heck, you'll get cramps all over. But you'll also lock into a rhythm, a pace; and once you do, you'll learn how to push past the pain. Then, when you finish, you'll feel great. It's amazing to know that you endured and finished the race!"

Many Christians jump into ministry or organizational leadership without having been adequately warned of its pitfalls, potholes, and process. It's like thinking you're about to run the 200-meter only to discover that you're actually in the marathon. There's a horrible pain under your ribs, and you're only at mile two! Like me, if you're aware of certain aspects of leadership, you too can run "the race set before you" and finish strong "according to the grace given to you." When you understand the process of becoming the leader God intends you to be, you'll be much more likely to endure that process instead of quitting. When you realize that God is more concerned with your becoming like Jesus than your becoming successful, the process truly begins. Then, you're on the path to joy!

It seems that the more I read about the biblical heroes of the faith or modern-day leaders in Christianity, the more I see that their lives seem to follow a pattern. It's like they go through certain seasons or stages before attaining influence. We won't all have the same level of influence, because our individual race is unique to us. It's distinctively ours to run. However, God does want to teach us all the same lesson: the joy of sonship.

The Holy Spirit put this book in my heart to encourage you to let God do His work in you by learning from those who've gone before you. Every Christian leader who has come to a place of influence has gone through what I call "The Process." My goal is to take a look at a few leaders in the Old Testament—to identify the process they endured so they could see the Lord's promise to them come to life! I pray that you realize what they came to realize—Christian leadership is first and foremost about sonship.

In today's culture, all too often we see leaders put projects above people, bottom lines above relationships. Usually, that's because the leader has yet to value sonship above all. I want this book to inspire you to reach higher, but more than that, I hope it reminds you of what's most important in life. After all, if we can see the process for what it is, we're more likely to endure it and reach the finish line. Like in Matthew 25:21 (ESV), I want Jesus to say to me, "Well done, good and faithful servant. Enter into the joy of your master!" That is true success!

I want you to *know what it takes* to not only lead at the top but to stay at the top *and* keep your friendships and your family. Those are *not* worth sacrificing on the altar of success. God wants you to succeed. God wants your marriage to succeed. Sacrificing your marriage on the altar of success is not okay and that's not what God wants.

God wants you to make it as a leader. Satan doesn't. Satan wants to take you out. He wants to take me out. Why? His enemy is God, because he wants to be God; the Bible makes that clear. So why would the devil mess with you? Because you are God's prized possession—His "special creation," the Bible says. In fact, you are the image of God on the earth. So wouldn't it make sense for

Satan to take out his anger toward God on you? You need to know who you are and understand the value you have as a special creation of God.

If you're called to leadership, the target on your back is big. Satan doesn't want you to know who you are, how loved you are by *Abba*, Father God, and the power of God within you! You have the capacity to impact others for the kingdom of Jesus, make history, build the kingdom, *and* find joy in it! You have the potential to live out Father God's dream for your life and impact nations! You have miracles in your future! Jesus has promised to be with you, empower and comfort you, and partner with you in bringing heaven to earth.

Nothing is more meaningful than building God's kingdom using the gifts God's given you. If you're tired of the status quo and dwelling on the problems that keep you up at night, and if you desire to endure to the end and *not* have an asterisk by your name, *The Process of a Leader* is for you. If you're ready to live a meaningful life and lead others to do the same, read on.

CHAPTER 1

The P.R.O.C.E.S.S.

In my dad's generation, it was Jimmy Swaggart. In my generation, it's been Bill Hybels, Carl Lentz, or even theologian Ravi Zacharias. These men impacted millions for Jesus Christ. They likely started out on fire for God with hearts of integrity, but their moral failures not only saddened the body of Christ but also undoubtedly led some astray. The sad part is that there are countless men and women in between who quit the ministry or quit being Christian leaders for any number of reasons:

- » They fall into a trap set by Satan and lose their integrity.
- » They get too tired and burn out, not knowing how to say "no."
- » They begin to trust themselves instead of God and forget their place.
- » They believe that they *are* what they *do*.

Think of this book as a guide on how to finish strong. It invites you to trust God all the way through the P.R.O.C.E.S.S. of a leader. It aims to inspire you with stories of others who've paved the way, blazing a trail for you to have faith. We are standing on the shoulders of men and women who trusted God despite all the naysayers, critics, and skeptics. Because of their faith, we now follow Jesus. Because of their courage, we now have learned to put our trust in God and His holy Word. If my dad and mom hadn't given their lives wholeheartedly to Jesus over thirty years ago and faithfully served Him ever since, I wouldn't be the man I am today. My wife, our four daughters, our foster child(ren), my three sisters and their children, and hundreds in our area have been impacted by my parents' faithfulness. Since you're reading this, you too have now been impacted by Mark and Pam Biel.

I want to ask you: Will you finish strong? Will you let the Holy Spirit do His work in you? For whom will you pave the way?

THE VIEW IS WORTH THE CLIMB

In 1953, something remarkable happened: the first two people to ever climb to the top of Mount Everest made their mark in history. Edmond Hillary and Nepalese Norway reached the top at 11:30 a.m. after weeks of climbing. Their trek was fraught with difficulty. Anyone who climbs above eight thousand feet can get mountain sickness. There's the obvious danger of falling to your death. The bitter cold took the lives of many who had tried before them. Because food sources are rare on the climb, teams must plan, purchase, and then carry all of their supplies with them. Most teams hire Sherpas to help carry their supplies up the mountain, and Nepalese was one of them. Edmond and Nepalese planned for months, recruited a team of eleven physically elite candidates, and established nine camps.

Theirs was an incredibly dangerous mission. Two men before them reached three hundred feet below the summit but had had to turn around due to a snow storm. Edmond and Nepalese enjoyed the view at the summit of Everest, but only because they didn't give up during the climb.

Now, think about this: they were on the top of that mountain for fifteen minutes. Fifteen minutes! It's reported that they said the view was "worth it," and I believe that. But listen, Christian leader! We're going to be in heaven much longer than that! Heaven is eternity, and based on what Jesus teaches in His Word, how you spend your life here affects your experience there. Your view in the New Jerusalem will last for decades—eternity! The climb of becoming the person God wants you to be—becoming like the Son—is worth it! The view will be worth the climb. You will be in the presence of Jesus, worshiping Him and ruling and reigning with Him. Don't you think we should do everything in our power to give it our all while we have this life—what David calls "a morning mist"—on earth? There's a process to this climb, involving treacherous paths with cliffs on either side, but you will hear a voice behind you according to Isaiah 30:21 (ESV) saying, "This is the way, walk in it," as the Holy Spirit guides you into all truth.

Trust God and truly hear what you're about to read, and you'll get to the end of your life as a leader knowing that you impacted culture for Jesus Christ in a profound way without losing your salvation, your family, or your integrity. *That* is something to aim for! So, what's the process?

There are seven stages in the P.R.O.C.E.S.S. of a leader. They are:

P—*PROMISE*
R—*REALITY*
O—*OBSTACLES*
C—*CHARACTER TESTS*
E—*ENDURANCE*
S—*SUCCESS*
S—*SONSHIP*

We'll peel back the curtain of history and take a close look at the lives of some of my biblical heroes and find ourselves in their story. Their fears are our fears. Their beliefs and thoughts are a lot like ours.

I'm believing that God is speaking to your heart and drawing you closer to His. We're going to see the process of a leader play out in the life of Joseph and Gideon, and then in the life of our Lord, Jesus. We'll be made aware of where we are in the process of becoming a leader—namely, the leader God wants us to be. Anyone with influence is a leader. Do you have influence over a group? Then you're a leader. Do you want to have great influence, remain in leadership, and lead the way GOD intends you to lead? Then read on. That's the aim of this book.

Every leader whom God raises up in the marketplace, in the ministry, or on the mission field will go through a similar process. What determines who will complete the process and remain a leader? How is influence measured? Why is integrity so important to leadership? And why is it important to know the process? This is what we're going to discover together.

Like the cross country race I mentioned earlier, if you don't know the process, then you won't endure the process. If you don't endure the process of leadership, you won't truly become the leader God intends you to be—the person God wants you to be. You may fall far short of the potential within you. I want to help you endure! I want to encourage and equip you to fight the good fight and *finish* the race. There's no reason you should get to the end of your life and have any regrets. Sure, we'll all have a few. But too many Christian leaders have started out strong and then had a major blunder, and that doesn't have to be your story. Too many leaders have potential, stored-up energy, and power given by the Holy Spirit that never gets used—and then broken lives remain broken. You can reach the pinnacle of your full potential without compromise. It can be done. I've seen it.

I'm not saying you'll be perfect. Only Jesus is perfect. But you can learn to submit to the Spirit of Jesus who will purify you and empower you to build His kingdom. More important than the leader you'll become is the person you'll become in the process. That's what God cares about most—your heart. Sadly, too many leaders worry only about the destination or next quarter's goals and never pay attention to their own heart and the person they're becoming. God cares more about friendship with you than blessing you with success.

What matters most to the Lord is that you develop a love for Him so that, like David, you can say, "In my integrity, you hide me in Your presence (Psalm 41:12)." That friendship with God, that kind of relationship, happens when you are willing to go through the process. Knowing Jesus is the treasure!

Once you go through the process, it will, of course, be repeated throughout your life. You'll again face obstacles—problems you and your team need to solve creatively with the help of the Holy Spirit. You'll undoubtedly face character tests. You and I will be tempted until the day we go to be with the Lord to give up in moments of weakness and temptation, to give glory to ourselves instead of God to whom all glory belongs.

I just want you and every young person to be able to say like the apostle Paul in 2 Timothy 4:7 (NIV), "I have finished the race. I have kept the faith." I want this for myself. Paul, in essence, was saying, "I have completed the process of being poured out for Christ. I've come as close to knowing Christ on this side of heaven as possible." I pray that we will able to say the same thing when our days are near their end. I pray that we keep a pure heart, knowing we've obeyed the Master in everything He asked of us.

PROMISE | Reality | Obstacles | Character Tests | Endurance | Success | Sonship

PROMISE

First, God gives us an amazing promise. For each of us, it's a little different. If you're like me, you had a moment (or two) where God spoke to your heart and gave you a glimpse into your future—a future that would honor Him and make your life meaningful and significant. Many of us have had numerous encounters with the Lord in which His Spirit has deposited a promise in our hearts.

All of us want our lives to be meaningful. Many people assume that this sense of meaning, happiness, or joy will come from achievements or by "climbing the ladder." While this book does give some advice on how to be more effective, that's not what it's about. It's about the heart. A life that is meaningful is one that is spent serving God by serving others and believing His promises. You won't feel that your life is meaningful because of a certain balance in your bank account, or when you are finally given *that* position. Life takes on true meaning and joy when you know Jesus Christ personally and step into your calling—the promises over your life. Before we step into that calling, God has to do a work in our hearts.

This promise God has given you (or is going to give you) is special and unique—different than mine, your parents, maybe anyone you know. One of the first pitfalls we can fall into is chasing after another person's promise. Only God can give you your identity—no man, no company, no ministry or minister can give it to you. Your calling and promise are unique. How do you find it?

Your promise is often related to a conflict in your heart. Why?
Your calling is often related to your conflict, your problem.

llllllllllllllllllllllllllllllllllllllllllllllllllllllllllllllllllllllllllllllllllllllllllllllllllll

What problem bothers you the most, keeps you up at night, and causes you to say to yourself, *Someone needs to do something about that*? That "someone" might be you! That conflict is an indicator of the area you're likely called to and it's leading you to a promise God wants to give you—a promise He has planted in your heart—for the benefit of others!

A PROMISE IN MY LIFE

I remember standing in a Christian music store (remember when we had those?) in 2004 in Pensacola, Florida. On one of the TVs, a service was playing of a live album recording at Hillsong. I remember standing there. All I was doing was wasting time, because I was going to be thirty minutes early for work. Next thing I know, I was crying in a bookstore. God gave me a "suddenly" that I wasn't expecting. There was already an ember burning in my heart—a desire to write songs that people could use in worship. That's a big reason why I was attending Bible college at the Brownsville Revival.

I looked at the TV and saw someone kneeling down in this huge auditorium filled with people worshiping Jesus and singing about their love for Him with passion. I suddenly heard the Lord say loud and clear, *I'm going to do this in your life, if you'll let Me. I'll give you songs for the nations.* I was in tears, shocked. I certainly didn't know what all that meant. I still don't know all that it means. I just know that God gave me a promise that day. It was echoed over the years in other situations in which prophetic words were given to me: promises that God was going to use me, my music, and my instruments. All of these words were from people who didn't know me.

I felt totally inadequate because I had failed five auditions to be a worship leader! I was not feeling confident about that sort of calling. To be honest, I was getting close to quitting. Nonetheless, the promise was there, whispered to my heart with the booming voice of a gentle Father. Two decades later, I've had the opportunity to lead people into worship to Jesus and it's one of the most beautiful things in life. To hear people pour out their praise to Jesus, the Lamb of God, and to sense His nearness—there's nothing like it! God made good on His promise despite my insecurities and fears!

I've written down many of the promises *Abba* Father has given me in a document called "Journal with Jesus." Some of them have happened right in front of my eyes, and some are yet to come. I hold on to those promises that are yet to come with total assurance that God is going to bring them about, not because of my abilities but because of His! I know that He is the Author and Finisher of my faith.

He who began a good work in me will bring it to completion on that great day.
—Philippians 1:6

I pray about my role in these promises and wrestle with God as Jacob did. Like Jacob, I often walk away with a limp. More people need to walk with a limp—an unsettling need to contend with God for His purpose to be fulfilled in their life.

I'm learning just like you are. I'm leaning in to hear His voice, and sometimes His voice scares me! Later in this chapter, I'll share with you about our church planting vision and how God spoke to me through people. God shared a promise that shook me to my core and tested my faith. God is now fulfilling that promise right before my eyes!

My wife, Danielle, received this word about being a mother over and over in the last few years. What did God do next? God put a burden for foster care in both of our hearts. We suddenly felt *this* was a problem that had to be solved. We had a conflict in our hearts as we thought, *These kids shouldn't have to endure feeling unwanted or even neglected.* That sense of conflict, that feeling of, *This isn't right,* led us to our calling. You, too, have a calling, and it's connected to a conflict in your heart.

Too many leaders are settling in, content with the status quo, leading with the wrong motivations. They lead from a place of obligation, guilt, duty, or, even worse, greed. These motivations may even be lurking within your own heart.

Even if you see a level of success in your current leadership, I would ask you this: is God pleased? Are you being faithful to what *He* asked of you? Will you be able to stand before Jesus one day with a clear conscience that you led for the right reasons—to serve Him and to extend His family? Will you be able to confidently say that you stepped out in faith to do impossible things with the Lord? This book aims to get your heart to that place, so you can lead from a place of promise, endure, have joy, and live from the identity of sonship. That must be your *why*. It's the only *why* that doesn't fade.

GOING NOT KNOWING

I've often asked God what I'm supposed to do to be obedient to His call regarding a word from Him. Then, I do my best to walk in obedience to His voice. Like Abraham, we often "go not knowing." I want to have that kind of faith. Don't you? The faith that compels me to just pack up and walk if God tells me to walk. Sometimes, I wish God gave us a GPS and a detailed route! He doesn't, though.

I want to dream in the face of fear. I believe that God is faithful to fulfill His word over my life, and I refuse to accept average as normal. Normal faith in Jehovah God and His beloved Son Jesus will take us on adventures we didn't anticipate and to summits where we'll enjoy the view of His majestic design.

Faith in the God who merely spoke the earth into formation won't allow me to settle for average or accept a mundane Christianity as "normal."

In a moment, we'll look at the story of Gideon, and we'll see the battles that were won! I may sound a bit like a ten-year-old, but maybe it's time we become childlike again. Maybe I'll pick up some superhero jammies to inspire me. Maybe you should, too. Adventure awaits! Before I tell you about Gideon, I want to tell you about a beautiful memory with my kids.

BURIED TREASURE

Selah, Elli, Eva, and Eden, my four little girls, could hardly contain their excitement! I had taken a wooden microphone box and placed all kinds of treasures in it! Chocolate. Suckers. Stickers. It was filled with treasures! I had taken a compass and plotted a course on a map that led through the woods behind our house, over the creek, and straight to a buried treasure. When I told them about this buried treasure and handed them the map along with the compass, they lit up in anticipation! "Where is it? Where is it?" they shouted. I said, "You have to follow the map and use the compass. The map will tell you what landmarks to look for. The compass will tell you if you're going in the right direction, and I'll come behind you and speak up if you get lost or confused." They ran off in a hurry, to which I shouted, "Wait! You have to look at the map!"

They slowed down, found the treasure on the map, and said, "There it is!" They fought over the compass before finally agreeing to a plan. They went southwest for thirty steps and looked for the mossy tree. They went too fast a few times, and I had to speak up and tell them to pay attention and nudge them in the right direction. Once they found that huge X in the dirt, they shouted and started digging with sticks. One of them started digging with her hands! They opened the buried treasure and split the loot. It was a memory we'll share forever!

That buried treasure is like the promise of God on your life. Your calling is there. You know it. You know there's a divine purpose for your life and you want to find it! That map is like the Word of God. If you'll pay close attention to it, you'll be on the right path. That compass is like the Holy Spirit nudging you in the right direction.

He'll speak up when you're a little off-course. He'll not only use trusted people to nudge you when your character needs correction, but He'll also speak to you regarding your next step. Don't run ahead. Slow down and listen for His voice. As my girls' father, I felt incredible joy guiding them. I knew that they could do it! I knew if they paid attention to the map, the compass, and my voice, they'd reach that treasure and have a blast!

God the Father has great things in store for you! There's joy in discovering purpose that only comes in the journey. You'll grow fonder of your Father's voice and, in the end, love Him more than the treasure.

ALL GROWN UP

Many Christian leaders are all grown up. There's no more time to be curious like a child, to ask, "Why?" and "Why not?" There's too little grace for risk-taking or mistakes. Everything is safe. Every dollar is accounted for. Every move is measured. Every person is safe at the company, at the church. And everyone is . . . bored. What happened? We got all grown up—that's what happened. We forgot to dream and be curious like children. We forgot sonship: that our Father is unlimited, He wants a big family—complete with crazy uncle and smelly grandpa—and Jesus invites everyone to the party: the hustler, the homeless, and the holy.

We forgot how to be curious and childlike. We forgot that our Father is unlimited. We forgot that our Father wants a big family—complete with crazy uncle and the smelly grandpa—and Jesus invites everyone to the party: the hustler, the homeless, and the holy.

IIIIIIIIIIIIIIIIIIIIIIIIIIIIIIIIIIIIIIIIIIIIIIIIIIIIIIIIIIIIIIIIIIIIIIIIIIIIIIIIIIIIIIIIIIIIIIIIIIIIIIIIIIIIIIIIIIIIIIIIII

We've been so busy working for God that we haven't spent time with and in awe of Him. It's like we've forgotten who He is: a loving Father who gives promises to His children, who wants to be Father to so many more, and who wants you to extend the invitation by using your unique personality and gifting. He has a promise! In time, God will fulfill His promise. He does it, though, in HIS timing, not ours.

In Luke, when the angel showed up in young Mary's home, God was giving quite an update as to His plan and promise being fulfilled. The long-awaited Savior was going to be conceived in *her,* and she would bring Jesus into the world! WOW! What a promise! What a miracle! God wanted to add another layer of assurance to His promise: "No word from God will ever fail" (Luke 1:37, NIV). What a promise and what an exclamation! You can almost hear the confidence in the angel's voice!

Before the promise is seen, there's a process.

Promise | **REALITY** | Obstacles | Character Tests | Endurance | Success | Sonship

REALITY

After we get a promise from the Lord in prayer, we start to feel reality set in like a cold, heavy blanket. We begin to doubt ourselves. All the reasons that Satan is giving us for why we shouldn't even begin are starting to make a lot of sense. We normalize our victimhood.

The reality is that we can't get to where we want to go until we come to grips with where we are. It's been wisely said that the number-one job of a leader is to define reality. People often know there's a problem, but they have difficulty defining it or its root cause. You can't overcome an obstacle or defeat an enemy you haven't defined. Leaders do that—with all the ugly facts involved.

Leaders who won't get honest about the complications facing their organizations are seen as too optimistic. They won't admit to morale being so low within their teams that the last product launch bombed. They simply gloss it over with overtly positive comments and empty metaphors. They blame it on "the culture right now" or the team member who didn't work hard enough. If you only paint a pretty picture, avoiding any facts regarding real problems, your optimism is seen as flaky. People are looking for leaders who will define reality and propose a plan to change it. They are observing, watching, to see if you're honest about the problems you and the team are facing. Your team is watching you. If you're not honest with the obvious problems, their level of trust in you goes down. Trust is built when leaders not only have a promise and vision for the future but also a willingness to define reality and the steps needed to overcome it.

You also must face the fears you carry within your heart. We don't want to admit our areas of weakness or where we need to learn and grow. If we admit where we are weak, then we look *less* like a leader, right? If we "show our cards," we look like weak leaders, right? The ironic thing is that we are at our best when we will admit our worst. The people you love want you to be REAL. When surveyed by the Townsend Leadership Program, the majority of employees polled said that they would rather have a leader who is honest than perfect.

Define where you are *now*: what you believe now and how it may be hindering your leadership. This is the first thing a leader does—face the demons within. It's like when you want to travel somewhere. In the age of iPhones and copycats, we all have a GPS or a Maps app. The app simply won't give you a route to reach your destination until you allow it to locate your current location. In fact, "enable location services" is one of the first steps we all take when we get a new phone or install a new app. Why? You can't reach your destination until you are honest and clear about where you are *now* and the problems that surround you.

As pastors and leaders, we're constantly in the position of helping others grow and reach their personal goals, marriage goals, etc. Because of this, we can begin to assume a lie: we've got it all together; we've arrived. The truth is that we still have fears that, like a strange thief, disguise themselves as "wisdom" and break into our hearts to try to make a home there. The truth is that, without Jesus, we are a dumpster fire!

The truth is that our company's systems and operations can improve. Our church's plan for reaching people, making disciples, or making disciples who make disciples can improve! Our company can become better and more competitive. We can always improve and learn. If you feel you don't need to learn or change, then *that* is your first problem.

Just because you see problems doesn't mean you misunderstood the promise. With every promise from God comes problems to solve. That will require humility—from you and your team.

Learning and making needed changes can be the most fun and rewarding—even unifying—steps you and your team make together. But if you won't face reality, then you won't reach your final destination because you can't determine a route—a course of action—until you "enable location services" and establish *Where We Are Now as an Organization.*

I want to give a shameless plug for my next book, *Leverage Leadership.* It'll help you establish reality—where you are in relation to your vision (where you want to be as a company or ministry). This book, of course, is not about systems, teams, and organizational health. It's about personal health. It's about you. Yeah, the one in the mirror. The one who gets up early every morning to lead the charge and tackle the day.

REALITY REQUIRES OBSERVATION

Observation is hard today because we live in such a distracted world. Leaders never make an impact because they don't even know the reality around them—they're not observing because they're too distracted by their phone or their agenda. Slow down. Observe. Face reality. Facing reality is about being honest. This stage requires honesty and observation. Observation can be overlooked (don't miss that pun … it's funny yet true.)

In today's world, observation is at an all-time low. We're constantly bombarded with screens and information. If you can't stop and put your phone down long enough to look around you and see the culture and its moral trends, you won't ever begin your leadership journey. If you don't take the time to pray in the morning and ask God to show you the reality of the genuine pain in those around you, then you won't do anything about it. If God's stirring your heart regarding the pain of those being trafficked, don't ignore it. Don't numb the voice of the Holy Spirit with just another episode on Hulu or Netflix. Stop the entertainment, social media, and email. Close your eyes and think, *Lord, what's my reality? What's a problem facing me and my friends spiritually? What's the reality of my own heart? Is there jealousy? Do I wish I had . . . do wish I were . . . ?* What are you afraid of? Stop reading the book and ask yourself, *Is there anything I'm afraid of? Am I afraid of not . . . ? Am I afraid of becoming . . . ? Am I afraid of being replaced because . . . ?*

THREE REALITIES

You've got to face three realities if you want to reach your full potential as a Christian leader:

1) I'm Still Growing.
2) Our Team Can Do Better.
3) My Promise Is Unique.

THE FIRST REALITY—I'M STILL GROWING

You have issues. I do, too. I'd like to say that I don't. But that's not reality. I do. I have insecurities. I have moments of weakness. I have thoughts that cross my mind that I wish hadn't. If you say, "Weird. I don't," you're not facing the first reality. What I recommend you do is ask people who work with you every day a few questions. That is, of course, if you're brave enough. You know, if you're not "chicken." See what I did there? I appealed to your ego to get you to do it. Hey, whatever will get you to face reality.

Questions for Colleagues and Friends

Is there a bad habit in my life that bothers you? I want you to be honest with me, because I'm learning that I can't grow as a person or leader if I'm not willing to face reality—and that includes any bad habits that I have.

Do *not* defend yourself when they respond. I was given this advice in a marriage class at our church, Rock of Grace. It was so helpful to my marriage that I figured it could be applied in work settings as well. Why not? Why not improve workplace morale by addressing any bad habits I need to break to lead others more effectively?

Is there an elephant in the room? Is there something you need me as the leader to address that I've been unwilling to address or maybe am even ignorant of?

Is there a way I can better lead you to make you successful?

Questions for God

Lord, is there any wicked way in me?

Are there fears within my heart that you want to remove?

His Holy Spirit will point out to you anything that isn't holy. Keep this in mind: if the Holy Spirit does correct you regarding a certain belief or behavior that isn't pleasing to Him, it proves that He loves you and that you're His! 1 John 1 and 2 tell us that when He corrects and reproves us, that shows us that He is our Father who loves us.

"Lord, I believe, but will you help my unbelief?"

» One of the greatest prayers every prayed came from a Roman official in the army. We can read the full story in Mark 9:14–30, but I'd like to summarize it. The disciples were unable to help a young boy who had seizures and was often burned by fire. The dad was desperate, and his faith had all but run out. If you had been asking God for a miracle for your child for 10 to 12 years and hadn't seen it yet, your faith would be on the brink, too. The boy's father was confronted by Jesus' declaration, "All things are possible for those that believe" (Mark 9:24). The father's response is beautiful. It's honest, yet hopeful. It's humble, yet confident: "I believe; help my unbelief" (Mark 9:25, ESV). Too often, we won't acknowledge our own struggle with doubt. Did you know God just wants you to be honest with Him? More than your perfection, He wants your honesty.

» In Hebrews 11, we read about every hero of the faith and how they believed in the promises God had given them. Even when it was hard, they believed, and that belief is connected to their righteousness. Did you realize that your belief is connected to your righteousness?

THE SECOND REALITY—OUR TEAM CAN DO BETTER

No more hiding in the winepress, hoping someone else will do something. Gideon was hiding from his reality, unwilling to face the facts. He was in such seclusion that God Himself visited Him to get his attention.

Isolation is not how God wants you to live or to lead. Isolation is a recipe for disaster. You were made for relationships, to grow *with* others, to come to their aid—and at times, to need their support. How can you do that if you're isolated, never willing to see the world or engage those around you? A true leader is never stuck in his office 9 to 5. People in your city, in your neighborhood, and on your street are suffering from a lack of hope or purpose, and you have the answer! You have Jesus! People on your team need to talk to you. You, as the leader, need to open the door to that conversation. Face the reality that, if you don't rise to your calling and begin to serve God where you are, others will suffer. Define reality. Let others help you.

The promise God has given you will never be fulfilled until you face reality. The reality of your insecurity will keep you from giving away authority to others. You'll crave authority instead of giving it away. The reality of your insecurity will keep you from taking risks—risks your church or organization needs to take. The reality of your inner demons, the fear that keeps you from even dreaming about growing your team, will limit your impact. Those fears, if ignored, will stop you from reaching your potential. Those realities of your heart need to be faced. It's time to look in the mirror and face reality. You do have what it takes! You just need to let God remove some of the garbage inside of your heart.

GOOD HATE

There is a good kind of hate. You've got to hate the problems in your current reality. If you don't, you won't do anything to solve them.

True leaders not only notice the problems but also have an emotional reaction to them. It's personal. They hate the effects of the problem and the way that it hinders people or keeps them imprisoned. The problem could be a mindset, a perspective. It could be political, physical, or financial. It could be a negative growing trend in society or even in your town. Regardless of what it is, leaders see not only the problem but also the long-term negative effects of that problem on real people who have hopes and dreams. Real leaders face reality and hate the problem enough to act.

Danielle and I believe that every child deserves a safe, loving home. We are committed to that. We are emotional about that. We are called to that. We're discovering our promise. We have a good hate. We hate that there are kids who are neglected or abused, and we hate that they often repeat the cycle. We hate how sin destroys a family. God put within us a table-turning mission: a mission to stop the generational curses and show kids and their parents what real love looks like. It's hard. It's exhausting. It's also the most meaningful thing our family has ever done. We didn't know all the answers when we started; we just started.

Real leaders act—*now!* They know that doing something is better than doing nothing and that the first step is the most important. Christian leaders are no different. They realize that they will never have all the answers before they begin. They simply begin, trusting God to fill in the gaps when needed.

YOUR PROMISE ISN'T FOR YOU

Keep in mind that, sometimes, you won't even see the full extent of the promise God's given you. Why? It's not so much for you. It's for others. Abraham was given the promise of a new land where his children and family would become so blessed and so extensive that they'd be hard to number! He didn't get to see the full extent of this promise fulfilled! Moses didn't enter the Promised Land. He had trouble with the character tests. He had trouble enduring and trusting God. He was used by God in incredible ways—don't get me wrong. But he did not enter the Promised Land. What if he had discovered that mentoring Joshua and seeing them all enter the Promised Land together was his highest privilege? As you go through the process of a leader, you realize that your leadership has very little to do with you. It has everything to do with them. God has a message of liberty for those you lead. You're just the messenger.

THE THIRD REALITY—MY PROMISE IS UNIQUE

You've got to take an honest assessment of the talents God's given you, begin to thank God for them, and use them to build His kingdom. Understand that your promise and purpose in life are uniquely tailored for you. The gifts God has given you are uniquely tailored for you to accomplish your promise! Many leaders fall short of their purpose because they begin to compare themselves to others. This is a classic trap of the enemy. Take ten minutes and read Luke 19:11–27. After you read, face the reality that is yours alone and answer these questions:

» What problems are around you?

» What is the conflict in your heart? What is it that makes you say, "That isn't right!"?

» What assignments has God already given you?

» What do you have in your hand?

You have something King Jesus can use! David had five rocks and a sling. Moses had a staff. Gideon had a horn. Samson had a donkey bone. Daniel had the gift of interpretation and wisdom. Esther had beauty and wit. Elisha had a mentor (and his coat). Peter had a big mouth. Paul had an amazing intellect and a gift for communication. Silas had the gift of prophecy. Martha had the gift of hospitality. Lydia had an entrepreneurial gift.

In the parable you just read from Luke 19, notice a few things about the servants and Jesus' response. Jesus rebukes them for comparing themselves to one another. He notes that the good steward is thankful to work, believes the master is kind, and gets rewarded in the end. The bad steward, however, resists submission and is ungrateful. He believes the master (God) is harsh. His mind is dominated by fear and, in the end, he loses what was to be his. What a stark contrast Jesus creates in this parable. Every leader should take note. We must be grateful for our obstacles, our opportunity to work. We must believe that God *is* good and that He knows what He's doing. We must believe that, if God put us in charge, then He believes we have what it takes. We must be motivated by love and not fear. The wicked servant said, "I was afraid, so I hid . . . ." Too many leaders are afraid—afraid of the outcome, afraid of what people will think, afraid of really letting God investigate their heart, afraid to face reality. After a leader faces the reality of their own fears and weak areas, they can more clearly see the obstacles standing in front of the promise being fulfilled.

Promise | Reality | **OBSTACLES** | Character Tests |
Endurance | Success | Sonship

OBSTACLES

Obstacles appear when we begin our leadership journey. What is leadership without leading people or teams over an obstacle? We've all been there, haven't we? Things are going great and then BAM! This happened to Moses. This happened to David. Out of nowhere, the contract is broken by the client or business partner. Our IP is stolen right out from under us. Our closest friend on the team goes AWOL—or worse, spreads dissension in the team, undermining our integrity or aptitude to lead. We'll look at some of those stories in this book. These obstacles are difficult. The new ministry program did *not* go as planned. The worship leader played in the key of B while the team played in B-flat for a solid minute because he put his capo on four instead of three (yup, I've seen it). The one person you delegated the most responsibilities to for the event simply didn't show up or call to cancel. The ministry or company website went down (and none of the data was copied and saved elsewhere).

Everyone hates an obstacle. Everyone. This may sound harsh, but hear me out—for simplicity and for the sake of understanding this stage, an "obstacle" can be a dilemma. I want to differentiate "reality" from "obstacle" briefly. Usually, a reality is something within, while an obstacle is something on the outside.

The truth is that an obstacle can only have two results—it can stop you or it can make you stronger. Period. If I'm on a path and suddenly have a 20-foot-long, 2-mile-wide wall in front of me blocking my path, I can stop in my tracks and quit. Or I can figure out a way to get over that obstacle. In doing so, I'm only going to become smarter or stronger or both. If I get a rope and climb over, I've built my arm muscles and have become stronger. If I get a plane and fly over, I've learned to fly. If I find a pilot to fly me over, I have a new friend. If I inspire a team to get over it together, I've made new friends and memories . . .

and probably had a few good laughs, too! If I quit, I fail. The adventure ends, and there's certainly no reward.

Every one of us on our quest for leadership will face obstacles. The sad thing is that there are leaders who quit at the smallest ones. Their journey ends just as it's beginning. They quit because they didn't respond correctly to the very thing God had given them to make them stronger or smarter.

A leader doesn't see an impossible obstacle when they see that wall. They see an opportunity. They see something to conquer. If you are naturally pessimistic, I encourage you to put on a different perspective: the perspective of faith. When you face a problem at work, address the problem and, yes, face reality; but then work hard at creatively finding a solution. In fact, any time you submit a problem to your boss, submit a suggested solution. Leaders turn obstacles into opportunities. That's not just "leader talk," either; that's what faith in God does.

**Religion focuses on what we can't do. Faith
focuses on what God can do and has done.**

||||||||||||||||||||||||||||||||||||||||||||||||||||||||||||||||||||||||||||||||||||||||||||||||||||||||||||||||||

But what do we do when that 20-foot wall is a person—when a person is the obstacle? Keep this in mind: a person is never the obstacle. Often, the disciples would say, "Jesus, make these people go home." In other words, "They're in the way." If people are in the way of your dream, then you've got the wrong dream. You've mistaken the pride in your heart for a promise from God. People will give you problems, there's no doubt about it. Even your own team may create obstacles for you. But *they* are never the enemy.

Jesus said, "If they hate Me, they'll hate you." If they lied about Jesus, they'll lie about you. If they were combative towards Jesus, they'll be combative towards you. Jesus knew that this was simply the sin within these individuals. If Jesus was able to forgive them and focus on their potential, then you can too! If Jesus was able to lead them despite the obstacles they provided Him, then He can help you lead them, too! Teammates will falter. Friends will walk away. Those you lead and serve may turn and bite you. Hurt people hurt people. Loved people love people. Know that those who seem to be creating obstacles for you may just need to know how deeply they are loved by Father God and even by you. Be reminded of how loved you are, and from that place of security, love and forgive people and keep leading them.

Promise | Reality | Obstacles | **CHARACTER TESTS** | Endurance | Success | Sonship

CHARACTER TESTS

Before Michael Hyatt was the CEO of Thomas Nelson and a best-selling author, he was a new staff member promised $27,000 with the understanding that he would get a raise of $3,000 after ninety days if he did well. He hustled and killed it. When the time came for the raise, the company instituted a wage freeze. His boss had such integrity that he paid Michael the $3,000 out of his own pocket. WOW! Now that's character.

Character is underpromising and overdelivering. Too many leaders make big promises and then underdeliver. That breaks trust, the bedrock of every relationship. Instead, when you are given an opportunity to commit, give it your all and overdeliver on what you've committed to do. Character is showing up on time or early, doing the right thing just because it's the right thing, and choosing to go the extra mile to do your part—even if others are being lazy. Character gives 110 percent and makes no excuses. Character means you say what you mean and mean what you say without being mean. You follow through and you can be counted on.

Character is a defining characteristic of every great leader. Without it, you simply will not last. People will only follow a leader they know they can trust—someone who is reliable and truly has their best interests in mind. When your team sees you pass a character test, it inspires them to keep following you. If you flunk a character test, admit it. Your team will forgive your mistake. They won't forgive your unwillingness to admit a mistake. Don't try to disguise your character flaw or mistake with charisma. Admit it when you could've done something better or when you missed the mark. Your team will value that honesty and that moment will, ironically, build more trust among the team.

Overcoming obstacles can soon become addictive. It can put a smile on your face—a good smile. You know the kind: when you've reached a goal or solved a problem in your church or company. The next week presents a new obstacle and God gives you wisdom to solve that, too! It's a joy to go to God in prayer, ask Him for wisdom, and then leave the prayer closet and get to work together!

The problem with overcoming an obstacle—or even many in a row—is that you're tempted to believe that you're invincible—that nothing can harm you. You can do no wrong. Nothing could be further from the truth. When you reach a place of success, when you overcome a big obstacle—be it through your own diligent efforts, team unity, even a stroke of luck, or simply the hand of God giving you a miracle—then you're tempted to think that *you deserve more* than you do. And this is where the next step in the process begins: your character is tested.

When you begin to think this way, the cure is gratitude. Gratitude says, "Everything I've been given is enough." It says, "I don't want more. I need less." Gratitude says, "Because I'm so thankful that God helped me reach this goal or overcome that obstacle, I'm going to remain humble and teachable. If He helped me with this, He can be counted on for wisdom again." God remains the noun, the one at the center, the actor with the lead role. Your character will also be tested the minute you overcome an obstacle or defeat a common enemy.

**Character is missing when you believe you
deserve more than you do—that your success
is only the result of what you've done.**

Satan wants you to believe that you succeed all on your own—that your success is man-made. You must recognize what a Christian leader recognizes: "Others paid the price for me to enjoy this moment of success." You did not arrive where you are on your own. Trust me. Someone taught you how to work hard, how not to steal or take someone else's credit, how to persevere. Someone likely created the environment in which you serve. Someone paved the way. Someone demonstrated for you what it means to lead well. Are you a pastor at a church? Someone planted it. Are you the new vice president of your firm? Someone started that firm. Are you the starting guard? Your coach saw your potential, gave you the disciplines to be fit enough to last the length of the game, taught you the plays, and put you in the game. Gratitude is a clear sign of a great leader who will increase his or her impact. It's a sign of character which leads to endurance. You are where you are as a result of your effort *and* the efforts of others. Never forget that.

When God gives you favor, be careful. With favor comes attention, and with attention comes temptation. Proverbs 16:18 (NIV) says it like this: "Pride goes before destruction; a haughty spirit before a fall." We've all seen it. Another leader becomes another statistic. Don't let that be your story! Guard your heart and remain humble and broken before God, ready for Him to correct you when you need it, knowing that He corrects His children whom He loves.

Jeremiah 50:32 (NIV) says, "The arrogant one will stumble and fall." Pride blinds you to your own needs, which are obvious to everyone around you. When you're proud, you're the only one who doesn't see it. Pretty soon, people simply don't want to be around you anymore. If this is the case, you've lost your influence and therefore your leadership. Find a place to get on your knees, humble yourself before the Lord, and allow His grace to give you a fresh start.

The Christian leader in danger of failing the character tests is the one who feels he will never fall. That's why 1 Corinthians 10:12 says, "Take warning unless you fall." Satan knows when to time his attack. He often gives his greatest blow just after a great victory. Every leader we read about in the Bible faced this.

Soon after Elijah defeated 850 false prophets, Jezebel had him running for his life and feeling suicidal. King David was experiencing victory after victory. In fact, he hadn't yet known defeat. Satan placed Bathsheba in front of him during this season of success. After the greatest revival to occur in the city, Jonah's character was tested with the lie of victimhood and self-pity. And after being promoted by Potiphar and overcoming obstacles, Joseph faced his first major test of character.

James 4:6 says "The Lord gives grace to the humble and resists the proud." In commenting on this scripture, K. A. Richardson says the following.

Quoting Proverbs 3:34, James recalled for his audience that God is determined to resist the proud. Those who wrap up their selfishness and self-sufficiency in arrogance will receive the full measure of divine rejection. Such is the universal announcement throughout Scripture and the extra-biblical writings. Pride is frequently listed among the human vices and is closely associated with the sin of envy. Earlier in James's letter the story of the proud rich and the envious church leaders and their followers (2:2–4) show both God's opposition to the self-promoting rich and their self-serving welcomers as well as God's preference for the humble poor. Pride stirs up the desires of all those who have succumbed to various temptations of the heart. Pride leads to boasting. The sin of haughtiness not only tends to boast in what it has and in its own life but even boasts in what it does not have and takes credit for someone else's accomplishments. Arrogance totally obscures the faith that trusts in things unseen, hidden in God.

On the other hand, God shows favor to those who humble them-selves. All of James's hearers were invited to join the ranks of the humble who trust in God. The term here for the 'humble' is rooted in the condi-tion of lowliness and poverty. Biblically, God is particularly interested in reversing the hierarchies of status in the world. This is why God has

chosen "those who are poor . . . to be rich in faith" (2:5). The close con-
nection between the condition of lowliness and the virtue of poverty is
reflected in the story of Saul wishing to make David his son-in-law in 1
Samuel 18:23. David's simple response was, "I'm only a poor man and
little known." But precisely this attitude, which he maintained in spite of
gross sin throughout his life, made David a man after God's own heart,
that is, favored, graced. David exemplifies what the proverb is intended
to teach: God is always ready to accept those who accept him and to give
them more grace. Should we sin that grace might increase? No! But grace
does more than meet the challenge of our sinful desires.[1]

Every great leader, whether Joseph or David or Gideon, knew that he was
but a broken human in light of a holy Creator God. Moments of weakness, in
view of poor choices, always bring this reality to the surface. Great leaders are
willing to recognize it for what it is and admit their sin and need for grace. Those
who don't admit fault simply won't last. Humility in a leader not only follows
the example of Christ but also attracts others, as it connects with them on a
basic, human level. When leaders act as if they've never failed, they distance
themselves from the team they lead and, because of that distance, can't truly
know the team or their followers. And when you don't know those you lead,
you can't lead them well.

In Donald T. Phillips's classic book *Lincoln on Leadership*, he writes:

By today's standards, the moniker "Honest Abe" might be considered
pretentious or even contrived. But the fact is that leaders who tell their
subordinates the truth, even when the news is bad, gain greater respect
and support for ideas than their less virtuous counterparts. Even
though he had some detractors, Lincoln attained success, admiration,
and a positive image by maintaining his integrity and honesty. Those

---

1   K. A. Richardson, *The New American Commentary: James*, vol. 36 (Nashville: Broadman & Holman Publishers, 1997), 181–182.

who questioned his upbringing and education, or even his political affiliations, tended not to doubt his integrity. Lincoln showed the same degree of fairness and decency whether disciplining or congratulating a subordinate. Emulating his style will earn leaders the trust and respect that ultimately fosters passionate commitment. This approach shows that the truth is a common denominator for all interactions, among any group, and with people of varying personalities.[2]

In my first book, *Truth & Love*, I stress the importance of being honest with others to form godly, lasting relationships. I'm so tired of seeing Christians, especially lay leaders, leave churches because they didn't know how to handle conflict biblically. As a leader, this is true on a much greater scale. If you can't be honest with your staff as to where they're not meeting expectations and yet speak in love, you're not yet leading like Jesus. Jesus was unafraid to correct His disciples. He was more concerned with His success in terms of obeying the Father in training up disciples than He was with simply being liked at all times. The same is true for you. Be honest. Be sincere. Teach your team the importance of being real and being humble. You will teach them best by displaying humility. When you've blown it, admit it. When you could've done better, admit it. Be eager to "own it" and show a desire to improve. They will follow your lead and you will all be better for it.

Be transparent. Admit mistakes. Apologize quickly. Compliment others. Don't take all the credit. Take responsibility. Real leaders do this and know that humility is required to pass character tests. If your perspective is blinded by pride, you won't even see the character tests for what they are; you'll succumb to temptation, thinking that you deserve whatever Satan is offering you. You'll think you deserve more than you do.

---

2   Donald T. Phillips, *Lincoln on Leadership: Executive Strategies for Tough Times* (New York: Grand Central, 2009), 56.

**Sonship is knowing that all the Father
has given is more than enough.**

||||||||||||||||||||||||||||||||||||||||||||||||||||||||||||||||||||||||||||||||||||||||||||||||||||||||||||

When you feel that you deserve more than you have, you've lost sight of the commandment, "Do not covet" (Exodus 20:17, HCSB). Coveting is wanting what isn't yours—what God hasn't given you. Forgetting the goodness of God will cause you to covet. Coveting will lead to sin—a failure of the character tests. As leaders, we are always pushing ahead and asking for more, but we need to be very careful to guard our hearts against asking God to give us something just because another leader has it. Coveting or wanting a platform the Lord hasn't given you or hasn't given you yet is a slippery slope. Instead, let gratitude fill your heart for what you've been given.

Being thankful for what God has given you will keep you out of trouble. Hear me, leader! Being thankful for what God has already given you—the job you have, the spouse you have, the home you have—will keep you out of trouble. Thankfulness is like having a tour guide through the precarious land mines of character tests you're bound to face.

How many more headlines do you need to read to believe me? When a leader rises to the top, then has an affair, being duped by Satan into believing that he or she deserves more than they have, we all feel a little pain. The entire body of Christ feels that pain. We feel for the woman who was committed to him in marriage. We feel for the kids who have to suffer now, watching their parents fight and possibly separate. So much pain comes from a leader's moral failure. That failure began when the leader assumed that he deserved more. Wanting to make a bigger impact for Jesus is one thing; feeling that you deserve more is another.

Success is that feeling we get when we've overcome obstacles. Success is no more deadly than when it's in the public eye. When a man or woman is complimented over and over, it can soon "go to their heart," not just their head. When that happens, soon what was once off-limits is now okay. What was once "No!" is now "Maybe it wouldn't hurt."

Leader, don't forget who made you. Don't forget who called you out of darkness and into His glorious light! Don't forget that Jesus paid a terribly high price to redeem you and to restore you to friendship with God! Don't forget who you really are—a child of God, a prodigal come home, a cherished son of a loving Father. If you forget that, you'll strive to make your name great and, in that aim, compromise and fail the character tests. On the flip side, if you remember who and whose you are, you'll make it! Remember that Creator God created you and thereby has the final say on your intrinsic value, and you won't strive for another accolade or feel the need to be seen as something you're not. Find joy in simply knowing Jesus and being close to Him. If you'll discipline yourself to fuel that relationship by meeting with Jesus each and every day, opening His Word and "hiding His Word in your heart," you'll be able to "keep yourself pure" as the psalmist said—and you'll be glad you did!

Why does God even allow for these attacks or tests of our character? I think we need to be reminded of two things. First, God's Spirit is able to use anything to continue to purify us as the bride of Christ Jesus. One of the Spirit's primary roles is to find and prepare a bride for Jesus. Jesus used this metaphor of a wedding often. Apart from initially drawing men to Christ, the Spirit's next role is to continue to purify each person for the coming wedding supper of the Lamb. In the words of Paul, we are saved and being saved. So there's the purification aspect we can't forget. Second, we realize that, when our character is tested, we are strengthened as Christian leaders. We don't like the test, we don't enjoy it; but we are certainly stronger because of it. In the same way, an athlete doesn't so much enjoy the pains that plague his stomach as he runs eight miles during training. Yet every time he pushes past the pain, he's a stronger runner afterward. Your test makes you stronger.

Promise | Reality | Obstacles | Character Tests |
ENDURANCE | Success | Sonship

ENDURANCE

We *all* get tired sometimes. Every leader, even you, will face fatigue. You may be fatigued right now and not even know it. If you're lashing out at coworkers or staff, you may be fatigued. If you're blaming your short-tempered outbursts on someone's inability to perform, you're fatigued. If you find yourself demanding unrealistic performance from those you lead, you're likely fatigued and near burnout. You need rest. You need to find strength in spending time with Jesus.

I would encourage you to read an amazing book called *The Emotionally Healthy Leader* by Peter Scazzero. I require all our staff and campus pastors to read it. Why? Because in it, Scazzero describes in detail his life coming to a tumbling crash without his ability to see it coming. He describes the insecurities that plagued his heart and how we can surrender those to God and let Him become the focus of our lives. Go on Amazon right now and buy it. Don't worry, I'll wait.

You may know the story of the prophet Elijah feeling suicidal. He was hiding from Jezebel, who was chasing him with death threats. Now, you'd think that, after seeing God display His power with fire falling from heaven, Elijah would be celebrating on a mountaintop, right? No fear in sight, right? Nope. Although he was coming off a spiritual high, he was physically drained and needed a break. God brought him ravens with meat to nourish him. God forced him to nap. He didn't need another conference. He needed a nap and a meal. When's the last time you took a siesta? Do you realize that, sometimes, you just need a nap? As a leader, you're probably like me: driven and task-oriented. But with that drive, passion, and possibly a "go–go–go" personality, you must learn the discipline of rest. Your soul needs it. For your marriage, your relationship with your kids, and your ministry to be healthy, you need rest. For you to endure the process that God has for you, you need to rest.

In Elijah's encounter with God, notice this detail: ravens are meat-eaters. My friend in ministry, Andre Van Zyll, points out, "God will provide meat-eaters to not eat the meat so that you can get what you need. He loves you that much!" Sometimes, the most spiritual and efficient thing you can do is rest.

God designed rest into the order of the universe. He called it *Sabbath*. The fields yield greater crops when they rest every seven years. We yield greater energy and "performance" when we rest on the Sabbath and truly give the entire day to doing nothing except acknowledging that God is truly Creator and worthy of our worship and admiration. We get our emotional tanks refueled when we rest and take some "me time," as it's often called now. Me time isn't selfish. Taking time to close your eyes and enjoy the weather, a sunset, or a walk with your spouse is not only wise—it's honoring to God and it's obeying the order of life that He established. To endure the process of a leader, you must learn how to rest, for in rest, we are acknowledging the end of ourselves and the work of God despite the end of our energy.

FOUR WAYS TO PREVENT FATIGUE AND BURNOUT

1) Friends outside your ministry/company

Friendships that are authentic, honest, and fun are absolutely necessary for you to avoid burnout. A big part of refueling is being with friends who don't drain energy from you but add energy to you. You can feel it. I can feel it. We all know that feeling when we are drained after being with someone, be it a client or church member or anyone who simply needs you to help solve an issue. Yes, that's meaningful, but it's also draining. You need friends who leave you feeling reenergized after hanging out with them. There must be time when you're accomplishing nothing. Even if you have to reframe the hangout time, tell yourself that you're accomplishing the goal of being refueled by accomplishing nothing. Reframe the idea of downtime. You're not being lazy. You're refueling.

2) Hobbies

I had two mentors tell me the same thing when I became a lead pastor. "Jordan," they said, "Whatever you do as you enter this new season of becoming a senior pastor, do not quit making music altogether. You have to carve out time for that. Otherwise you'll suffocate." That was some of the best advice ever given to me.

I was writing and producing music three days a week for eight years before becoming lead pastor. Let's just say that "I LOVE MUSIC." There's nothing like it. To lock into a pocket and create a melody that rings in the ears of people, causing them to praise and be thankful, is simply amazing. I still make music every Friday, and I guard that time like a bulldog guarding a new bone. Why? I get to continue to be fully me. If you don't create some time for yourself to just enjoy something, you'll lose some of the joy in your life. It's a great idea to have a hobby outside of your church or business. Take time for something enjoyable that will give *you* fuel. If you "burn the candle at both ends," you'll burn out. That doesn't make you look spiritual, and burnout certainly isn't God's plan for you. It is not part of the process He has in mind and it's not what your spouse or children desire, either.

3) Daily Time with Jesus

Your daily devotional life must remain of highest importance. Without it, you'll begin to strive in your own strength and gradually depend on God less and less. This will leave you feeling worn out and burned out. Jesus died not to make you a successful leader. He died so you could be His friend and brother and know the Father on a personal level. This relationship of love must be preeminent. Nurture it. Guard it. Take care of your time with the Lord, and don't let any goal interfere with it. Don't let any demand from any person steal it. Don't let social media or the need to scroll keep you from knowing the One who holds the stars. Don't give up the inheritance for a bowl of soup. Value what Jesus paid for. Spend time daily with Him, and you'll find that you've got more than enough energy for the day and confidence to face what comes your way.

In the old covenant, there was a light in the tabernacle. When you look at the menorah and the function it served—to give light to the tent of meeting—you may notice that it had to be continually filled with oil from above for that wick to avoid burning out. Likewise, you are called to shine the light of Jesus Christ as a leader in your community; but unless you take time to let God fill you with the oil of His Spirit, you'll soon burn out. The wick needs the oil. Likewise, you need the oil of the Spirit, and that only comes through waiting and resting in God's presence.

Years after Moses and the tabernacle, we find David discovering the beauty of knowing God one-on-one. Let's follow David's example and discover the joy of knowing God intimately each and every day by spending time in His presence. No leader plans to quit or throw in the towel one day. We all want to succeed and put a smile on God's face. We want to endure. A key to endurance in your public ministry is your worship in privacy. Follow the apostles'example and take time to wait on the Lord to fill you and refill you on a regular basis. The leader who doesn't take time to pray and be filled is the leader who leads in his own strength, and man's strength will always come to an end. But in the Spirit, there is newness of life and an ease that enables you to keep going and keep going strong.

"It is not by might, nor by power, but by My Spirit," says the Lord. —Zechariah 4:6

||||||||||||||||||||||||||||||||||||||||||||||||||||||||||||||||||||||||||||||||||||||||||||||||||||||||||||||||||

4) Exercise

Do you want to endure? Take care of your body. The simple act of leading yourself, disciplining yourself into a routine of exercise, trains your brain to feel the following: *I'm in control of my life. My life is not out of control or out of focus. Other people and their demands are not dictating my every move. The Holy Spirit has given me the fruit of self-control, and He can help me with my health.*

It's so rejuvenating to work out and put your body in its proper place of health. Like most people, I'm not 100 percent diligent in this, yet I know that when I am, I feel much, much better. I've got more energy to lead and lead well. Thousands of studies have proven the various benefits of exercise. It increases your ability to think clearly, reach goals at work and, for most people, it leaves them feeling energized and ready for what lies ahead. Many of the greatest leaders of our day are also athletes or, at the very least, disciplined to exercise weekly. That's not a coincidence.

When your body, soul, and spirit are being taken care of, you're much more likely to endure the difficulties of leadership. You're more likely to manage criticism properly; and if you're a leader, criticism will come. It's an occupational hazard. If you aren't healthy and at peace—body, soul, and spirit—criticism will cause anxiety and lead to all kinds of trouble.

As a leader, not everyone will like what you say or the decisions you make. Know that up front. You're a leader. You lead. It's what you do. The very act of leading implies that you will be making changes. Maybe you've heard the old saying, "The only place that consistently rejects change is the cemetery." The people you lead are alive. . . . I'm assuming, anyway.

That said, there will be decisions you make that require them to change, and some of them simply won't like it. They'll criticize you. They'll tell you that you're wrong and may even say you're not hearing from God. Whether it's the wall color or a location change, those you lead won't always be 100 percent in consensus, and they may be critical of your decisions or even your motives. In those moments, don't get defensive or angry. Know that they are likely questioning only because they care about the organization you're leading. Now, if someone is simply critical or negative more often than not, you likely need to cut them loose. Some leaders don't have the courage to confront or release staff who are toxic and thereby they forfeit everyone's success. Those people need to go. And that's okay. Leaders need to endure, but I'm not saying that you should become a doormat.

The majority of time, those who offer critique are not being negative or rebellious toward you. Don't take it personally. They are simply wanting what's best. Be the leader who takes their criticism and questions and genuinely listens to their concerns with an open mind and heart. Endure criticism. Even welcome it. I've told my team often, "Tell me if I'm wrong or being unreasonable in any way," or, "Guys, let me know if you think that could've been better." I also ask, "Is there any habit I have that is frustrating you that you'd like to tell me about?" When given the permission, they'll sometimes share something that's a blind spot to me. I have even opened my sermon or lecture to my leadership team and asked some of my staff, "Please look this over and tell me what I'm missing or how it could be better."

Great leaders don't only endure criticism—they welcome it, because they want to be continually growing. After God gives you a promise or a dream, reality must be faced. In facing reality, there will be many obstacles to overcome and even tests of your character. If you endure these by humbling yourself and constantly looking to Jesus in prayer and to your team for feedback, you'll likely experience what the world would call success: a place in which you've either achieved your goals or have a following of some sort. For many, the stage of success can prove to be the most difficult.

Promise | Reality | Obstacles | Character Tests |
Endurance | **SUCCESS** | Sonship

SUCCESS

This is one of the hardest stages for any leader. Ironically, it's also the easiest. That's what makes it so hard. When you have success in the eyes of people, things start to get easier for you. People start to treat you with honor and respect, and the Bible teaches us to honor and respect those whom God has placed in authority, so that's fully expected. You may even get more perks now that you're "in charge." You may be commended so much that it goes not only to your head but also to your heart.

A crowd does not equal compromise. A crowd also doesn't equal true success in the eyes of God. Every leader is called to steward something unique.

||||||||||||||||||||||||||||||||||||||||||||||||||||||||||||||||||||||||||||||||||||||||||||||||||||||||||||||||

Keep in mind that not every leader who is successful is in error. It's very foolish and dangerous to assume that. There are many leaders who have a large following and are simply doing a great job with total integrity. Why do I share this? I share this because, for some reason, I'm seeing a trend in the last few years. Many pastors who have megachurches are attacked more and more. Often, their accusers are assuming something untrue. It's almost as if they assume that, if you have a large crowd, you must be compromising or be a false teacher. But if you go by that standard, Jesus would have been a compromising false teacher, and we know that's not true. So what is success? In the kingdom of God, it's obedience. It's faith. We know what it looks like in the world's eyes. We know that, to many people, success means moving up the ladder at work. It means reaching goals that you set out to reach. It means achievements, accolades, and being at the top.

In the kingdom of God, success is simply this: faithful obedience to God's voice.

||||||||||||||||||||||||||||||||||||||||||||||||||||||||||||||||||||||||||||||||||||||||||||||||||||||||||||||||

Earlier, you read Luke 19. Go back and ask yourself, *What stopped the servants from creating a return on investment for the Master?* Fear. Fear will always stop you from obedience, and obedience to the Lord is success in this life.

Success doesn't come after obedience to the Lord. We often think that success or failure is what is determined after we try. That isn't the case with God. Success or failure doesn't come after you try. The "trying" *is* the succeeding. The faith to say "yes" *is* the succeeding. Your success as a leader in the kingdom of God is determined by one thing and one thing only—humble obedience.

If you will simply obey God out of a true heart of thankfulness and love and let *Him* worry about the outcome, you'll begin to see miracles all around you as God moves in powerful ways! You'll see financial miracles for you and those around you! You'll begin to see your church, company, or nonprofit move forward with more progress than ever before. We as Christian leaders need to learn that big risks are all *small* risks when we serve such a big God!

The better you grasp your identity as a loved child of God, the bigger risks you'll take. To God, failure is never fatal.

The Gospels tell us that there was a man whose son was possessed by an evil spirit. It would throw his son into the fire, and he was constantly in danger. Can you imagine that fear as a parent? Can you imagine the worry you'd feel all day, every day? The man approached Jesus, probably thinking, *This is my last resort! Nothing else has worked so far!* "Nothing is impossible for him who believes!" Jesus said in Mark 9:23. Nothing is impossible!

If you say, "Well, our company morale is so messed up right now that it would take a miracle for it to change for the better," I have good news! Jesus still performs miracles! Begin to pray and ask God, "Lord, do a miracle at my work and turn the hearts of those who are angry and bitter into hearts of clay—humble and broken. I ask You, God, to do the impossible and turn our company around for Your glory! May every staff member and employee suddenly find the joy of working together to serve our customers! May each employee begin to thank God for their job and serve in their role with passion! In Jesus' name, Amen!"

If you're a pastor who's thinking, *I can't make any progress in this church. I've been praying for months, and nothing has changed*, pray again! Pray that God pours out His Spirit and revives hearts that are far from Him. Pray that God opens their eyes to see what's possible! God may not answer prayers like that until you pray and ask! God may not turn your church around until you simply ask Him to and believe that He will! God can do what seems impossible! And He can do it fast!

Ask the addict who was set free from the addiction through Jesus Christ in a Teen Challenge center. I've heard hundreds of men share about God's miracle-working power that set them free from cocaine, heroin, and alcohol addictions. I've seen them cry tears of joy describing how God took their desire for their drug away completely in an instant. God can do it! If God can deliver a man from an addiction, don't you think God can deliver a company from apathy? Pastor, if God can deliver an addict, don't you think He can deliver the members in your church? Believe Him for it! Ask Him for it! Believe it until you see it!

The trap many leaders fall into is the trap of success. They cling to approval, likes, listens, and views on their last video. If you're not careful, you'll end up checking how many likes you have on your last post—you know, to see if you're a valuable person or not. That may be blunt or a bit harsh, but if we're honest, we're all a bit insecure. We all, at times, crave attention or feel the need to be "liked." Pun intended. In our social media world, it would seem that our success can be quickly calculated by the number of shares, views, or likes on our posts. But is that truth? Is that how God sees us? Is that what God wants from us? Sure, making an impact on many people or more people is a great thing, but to crave or even to need to sense that we're "successful" is not what God wants.

God the Father doesn't want you to be successful—at least in the way the world defines it. God wants you to be successful in the way He defines it. He wants you to be significant, to simply be His son or daughter, to know how incredibly loved you are by Him. He wants you to comfort and love people in their time of need, expressing His unwavering Fatherly love for them. He wants His love to so fill you that you actually overflow with it. He wants your cup to run over with His goodness. When this happens—when you invite His presence to be the most important and the most treasured part of your life—you'll discover that your friendship is *significant* in the lives of people. You can only be significant in the lives of a few, even if you're successful in the eyes of many. Here is where you'll find your greatest joy and truest calling: just being loved as a son or daughter of God and then sharing that love with a brother or sister in God's family. Sonship is where it's at. As leaders in God's kingdom, we are sons and daughters aiming to bring more people into the family! We are aiming to bring more people into an awareness of Father God's love. Anything more than that is polluted.

Promise | Reality | Obstacles | Character Tests |
Endurance | Success | **SONSHIP**

SONSHIP

Being a child of God is the greatest joy and honor for us. If you miss this truth, you miss the meaning of life, and you'll miss the joy of leading people. If you aim for greatness as a leader but forget that you're first a child of God, you'll push people down to get to the top, only to find the top a very lonely place.

If you aim for greatness as a leader but forget that you're first a child of God, you'll believe the lie that you are great all on your own. You're only great because God made you great. You're only gifted because God gave you gifts.

If your joy and happiness in life are tied up in only your achievements, you'll be missing the joy God intends you to have—joy that can only come through relationship with Father God and relationships with your brothers and sisters in Christ. Life is about people, not projects.

You'll strive and strive, and although you'll hit goals, you'll be constantly longing for more. When you get a revelation of sonship, when you know that you're already completely loved by Father God, you'll have peace and contentment that last far beyond the goals reached or missed, the success or failure of a product or program. Ironically, the more quickly you understand this, the more risks you'll take, because when you know you're loved by Father God, no matter what happens, you're liberated to take risks!

Romans 8:29 (NLT) states, "For God knew His people in advance, and He chose them to become like His Son, so that His Son would be the firstborn among many brothers and sisters." I wonder, if we were more concerned with being a son instead of a success, how much trouble we would save ourselves. I wonder, if we leaders valued sonship and the heart of this scripture more than being "right" or "successful," how much more peace we'd have in our hearts and minds.

I remember a Saturday night when I was scared to death. It was late February, and that January I had just become the lead pastor of Rock of Grace church in Kinsman, Ohio. It's an amazing church that my dad and mom brought to a place of health over their twenty-six years of pastoring. I was going to share the vision for our church buying a building in a neighboring town to plant another church and, eventually, build a ministry training center called David University.

I remember thinking, *God, I've only been pastor for eight weeks, and they're going to think I'm crazy! Lord, what if I fail? What if they actually believe me and receive this vision, we buy a building, plant a church . . . and nobody comes!? Lord, what if . . . ?* These questions continued to race through my mind all the way until Sunday morning. I remember literally saying out loud, "I'm not going to say it. I'm not going to mention the buildings or all the ideas. I'll just mention a church. I've only brought it up it to a few people, so it's not a big deal." As I rambled on and on to the Lord telling Him why His plan wasn't going to work, all of a sudden, I heard the Lord interrupt my racing thoughts.

He said, *Jordan, you are my son. I'm going to love you no matter what. No matter if this fails or if it's a huge success, my love for you won't change. What we have together, that's not going to change.*

And I thought, *Wow, Father. You are so right! Why should I be so concerned with being a failure in the eyes of people if everything doesn't work out great? Why was that causing me to worry? Father, I'm at peace and full of joy just in knowing You!*

Why worry and fear about looking like a failure when Proverbs clearly tells us that the fear of man is a snare? When I feel that I've heard from the Lord, I want to come to a place where I just instantly obey and trust Him completely. I want to fully trust that He's able to help me accomplish what He's asking me to do. I think that's a big part of what faith means. I think that's what many of today's leaders are missing—the faith to believe the promise God's given them. Does God ever interrupt your racing thoughts of fear, worry, and self-induced anxiety? I hope He does. I hope you let Him speak as in 1 John 3.

Jesus is the one who made sonship possible! When God sent Jesus into the world to die for us, it was to rescue us from the sin that was leading us to eternal death. We were on our way to being separated from God and His light and life forever. But then Jesus came! Jesus is the "new and living way" and He's the only one who lived a sinless life; therefore He's the only one who could do what He did. He died in our place—my place, your place! Isaiah 53:5 (NIV) says, "The punishment that brought us peace was on him, and by his wounds we are healed." Inside and out, we who've accepted Jesus Christ as the one who saved us have been changed into a new creation! We have gone from enemies to friends and from friends to family!

We are the children of God! We sit as His table! He provides for us! He cares for us! He is our Father, our Abba, whom we love more than anything. Jesus has made that possible!

||||||||||||||||||||||||||||||||||||||||||||||||||||||||||||||||||||||||||||||||||||||||||||||||||||||||||||||||||

We are the children of God! We sit as His table! He provides for us! He cares for us! He is our Father, our *Abba*, whom we love more than anything. Jesus has made that possible! And here's the point I want to make: we did nothing to deserve sonship. In fact, we deserved death. We deserved eternal separation from God due to our sins and all the times we've chosen to be selfish instead of generous, rude instead of kind, and demanding instead of giving. Jesus earned it. Jesus paid it all. Jesus achieved this liberty from sin for us! Jesus endured the cross so that we could be adopted as sons and daughters of God Himself!

SONSHIP IS EVERYTHING

The ironic thing is that, although this is the "last stage" of a leader's journey, it should be the first also. Why? The culmination of our lives is to be children of God and to stand in that truth. This is who you are before you're a leader and before you're gifted. Sonship isn't achieved; it's received. It's a gift—a gift of identity given by our Father in heaven.

Before you're talented, before your awards or achievements, you are loved as a son or daughter of God; and that is the most invigorating, life-giving truth that brings meaning to your existence. If you miss this, you miss it all. If you are successful and achieve your goals and yet never find friendship and intimacy with God as Your Father, you've missed not only the meaning of leadership but also the meaning of life. If you make millions as a Christian businessman yet forget that you were blessed to be a blessing because your Father God is Abraham's Father God, then you will have missed it all. If you're a pastor and your church becomes a megachurch reaching thousands every weekend, and you buy into the lie that your identity and value are determined by the number of people listening to you, then you've missed it. Let God return you to the joy of sonship.

Maybe you started out on the right path, eager to please God, but when you began reading this book, you felt the unsettling conviction in your heart. Maybe you've begun to pray these brave prayers. Maybe you've found in the reflection that there are insecurities and fears that race through your mind daily. If this is the case, I encourage you to give those to the Lord and find your identity completely in Him and in Him alone. Find your identity as a leader first in sonship!

Abide in Christ alone. Don't try to abide in your position at work or your perceived place of success. Instead, find joy and rest in knowing that you are unconditionally, unequivocally loved by Father God, the One who made you. You are fully known and yet fully loved, Scripture says. Whether you "succeed" or not, God your Father loves you to pieces. Your picture is on His fridge!

Yes, He has "plans to prosper you and make you successful" as Jeremiah 29:11 says. Yes, He has plans to "make you the head and not the tail *if* you obey Him," according to Deuteronomy 28:13. While these things are true, God's first priority for you is your heart, not what your hand can build. He wants you to know Him! He wants you, like it says in Matthew 6:33, to make His kingdom *first* in your life! He wants to extend His love to the nations through you!

But before He blesses you, before He uses you, He just wants you to be His! More than anything else, He wants a genuine relationship with you. He wants to hear from you. He wants to know your concerns, what makes you tick, what your dreams are. He wants it all. He wants to talk with you. He wants to befriend you. This is why Jesus gave His life! He did it not just to give you eternal life *then* but to give you real life *now!* You can know God personally! Talk to Jesus!

UNIQUELY LOVED

I have four daughters. Yeah, pray for me. I'm already giving awkwardly long, scary looks to the neighborhood boys, trying to scare them away. I recently slowly cocked a long-barrel pellet gun in my driveway as they rode by on their bikes. They didn't know it was a pellet gun. Hey, it's suburbia. You do what you gotta do.

My daughters are each so different and so uniquely loved. I am IN LOVE with each of them. They are the joy of my heart! It doesn't change my love for them if they ever break a sports record or become a success in the eyes of people. It doesn't matter if they get a PhD. Would I be proud of them? Of course! Would I commend them? Of course! But would my love for them change? Nope. Not one bit. If they became a successful minister or leader or doctor or businesswoman, I wouldn't love them more. Their achievements have no impact on my love for them. Guess what? Even their biggest blunders will still have zero impact on my love for them. Why? They are my daughters! Period. When they know this, they can find so much joy and rest in that truth—the truth that Mom and I love and like them, no matter what happens. The same is true for you and me. Leader, you are liked and loved by God well before you do anything to impress Him. Your guilt and your goals have zero impact on God's unique and personal love for you. Zero.

While this book is going to encourage you to make a greater impact for Jesus, this impact must never be at the expense of sonship. In fact, it's sonship that becomes the cause of the impact. My goal is that your ministry and leadership take on a whole new motive. My prayer is that you are motivated to be a great leader not to impress God but to obey God. My prayer is that you don't aim to impress people or to appear great. But my prayer is that you are motivated to be a great leader simply as a response to Father God's great love for you and for the world. My prayer is that your motive changes to simply bringing more children into God's family.

APPLY IT

Group Discussion Guide | P.R.O.C.E.S.S. | Week 1

I'm asking that you take some time every week with a group of Christian leaders and discuss the questions below. There are some things we simply can't learn without the authentic community of other believers. As leaders or soon-to-be leaders, you'll be able to relate to one another in a unique way. Others have experienced a trial or life lesson that they can share with you. They have had a revelation of God's love in a different aspect than you have had—I'm certain of it. Discussing what we learn in each chapter will enable you to go further faster. You'll learn from one another's mistakes and mountain-top experiences. Don't skip the "Apply It" section at the end of each chapter, even if it means going through the questions alone with self-reflection.

There are three altogether, so I encourage you to set aside three times when you can gather for just 20 to 30 minutes to discuss with other Christian leaders what you're reading together.

» Do you agree that most Christian leaders go through the P.R.O.C.E.S.S. outlined in Chapter 1? Who is a leader you can name who went through the "process" before attaining the influence they have today? Describe what took place.

» Without delay, name a leader that you look up to—someone you respect the most. Now, going around the room, share the character traits that you like about these individuals. You may find that the same character traits that are in Jesus are those you aspire to the most as we read this book together.

» Let's make this personal. What part of the process are you in right now? There are times when we'll hit these different phases again and again. Is there an obstacle that you faced years ago that tested your character and integrity? Is there an obstacle you're facing right now?

» Why is it tempting to want to be known as "successful," and what is it about this that reveals our sinful nature? Why do we sometimes crave accolades, "likes," position, or power?

» In your group, read Matthew 4:1–11. Discuss what Satan offered Jesus and why. Is it possible that Satan was actually offering something to Jesus that was already His, given to Him by the Father? Satan offered Him what? Power? Fame? Satan tempted Him to "prove" himself. Jesus already knew His identity—a loved child of God!

» Ask someone in your group to read Luke 15, the story of the Prodigal Son. Consider the following questions: Why was the older brother mad? What did the father do to celebrate the son that came home? What does this tell you about God the Father's love for you? If you had to pick, which character in the story most resembles you and why? Do you see yourself as the forgiven and thankful son or the jealous older brother? Discuss this statement: Religion is when you try to earn what the Father has already given.

Action Steps

Which leader would your team enjoy following more: the thankful one or the religious one?

This week, I'm going to be intentional about telling my team members,

_____, _____, _____,

_____ that their success is my success. I'm going to ensure they know that I am more excited about them reaching their goals than I am about me reaching mine.

The leader I mentioned in question 2 is _____.
The reason I look up to them is because they are _____.
These are character traits that I am going to ask God to strengthen in me.

If I had to list where I am in the process of a leader right now, I'd say I am in the phase of (circle one).

P.R.O.C.E.S.S.
Promise | Reality | Obstacles | Character Tests | Endurance | Success | Sonship

CHAPTER 2

Joseph

The Lord was with Joseph and gave him success in whatever he did.
—Genesis 39:23 (NIV)

The story of Joseph is world-renowned. Millions of people who've never picked up a Bible have seen the Broadway musical *The Coat of Many Colors* or the Disney movie *Joseph*. We can assume much of the world is at least familiar with the story. I'm hoping we find ourselves in the story of Joseph. Then, we can find Jesus.

Joseph went through the process of a Christian leader and endured until the end. God used him in a powerful way, economically and spiritually. Joseph serves as a type of Christ, and we'll get into that soon. But for now, who was Joseph?

Joseph was the great-grandson of Abraham, the "father of faith," as he's often called. Abraham was given a promise by God that we read about in Genesis 15. This promise was carried on to his children and grandchildren. The promise was that God would give him an everlasting family, a dynasty, and an entire kingdom would come from *his* offspring. The promise was a blessing—an eternal blessing—from God! The crazy part about all this was that Hebrews 11:12 (NIV) says Abraham was "good as dead." He was incredibly old, so a promise of children was a stretch! His wife Sarah was well past the age of bearing children, so this would be a miracle if it were to happen! It was, and it did.

Abraham tried to rush the process by sleeping with his servant because He felt God was moving too slowly. It's never a good idea to rush the process that God has you in. His promise will be fulfilled in His timing. His schedule, His ways, and His choices are perfect. We need to do our part, yes, but we don't need to *help God*. We take initiative and step out in faith in one way or another, but in this case, the promise was for him and Sarah, and Abraham simply didn't wait. Generations of heartache have ensued.

Eventually, Sarah did conceive. She had Isaac, and Isaac's wife had two sons: Jacob and Esau. Esau was older, and in that culture, that meant he actually deserved the blessing first from his father. As their father approached death, Jacob tricked his elderly father into believing that he was Esau, and he stole the blessing away from his brother (we can't easily explain this in a post-Christian, non-Jewish American culture). Right after this took place, Isaac was approached by Esau, and Isaac realized he had blessed the wrong son:

> *Isaac trembled violently and said, "Who was it, then, that hunted game and brought it to me? I ate it just before you came and I blessed him— and indeed he will be blessed!"*
>
> *When Esau heard his father's words, he burst out with a loud and bitter cry and said to his father, "Bless me—me too, my father!"*
>
> *But he said, "Your brother came deceitfully and took your blessing."*
>
> *Esau said, "Isn't he rightly named Jacob. This is the second time he has taken advantage of me: He took my birthright, and now he's taken my blessing!" —Genesis 27:33-36 (NIV)*

Anger drove Esau to even want to kill Jacob. Rebekah told Jacob about Esau's plan and sent Jacob away to her brother Laban's house. Jacob went, and on his way, God invaded Jacob's earthly reality with a vision and confirmed that indeed the promise given to his grandfather Abraham now rested on him, according to Genesis 28:13–15.

You may also know that Jacob offered to work seven years in exchange for marriage to Laban's daughter Rachel. But the deceit that Jacob sowed was about to be reaped. After seven years of labor for Rachel, Laban got Jacob drunk on his and Rachel's wedding night and gave him Rachel's sister Leah instead! I can't imagine Jacob's confusion and anger the morning he woke up, expecting to see his new bride Rachel, only to discover her older sister Leah! By the way, the Bible says she was "weak on the eyes." That's the biblical way of saying, "Look, she wasn't pretty, okay?" I'm not being shallow here. I'm just telling you what the Bible says.

Despite all this Judge Judy-like drama, the blessing still rested upon Jacob. He worked another seven years to get Rachel. Jacob had twelve sons over the years, but it wasn't pretty. Read Genesis 30 and you'll see what I mean. Leah and a servant had given children to Jacob, but Rachel was barren for a season. When she finally gave birth to Joseph, he was favorited, for it was Rachel that had Jacob's heart. They finally had a son together!

JOSEPH'S PROMISE

These twelve sons became collectively known as the twelve tribes of Israel. Jacob moved back to the land he had fled, the land of Canaan, the land of his father. Jacob's favorite son, Joseph, was only seventeen years old when Joseph began to have prophetic dreams about his future. God was giving Joseph a promise!

Out of all twelve sons, Joseph was clearly his father's favorite. That can never be good in any parenting situation. To make it obvious that one child is favored above the others is just not a good idea. Yet God used Jacob's parenting issues to uncover His plan of redemption. God always seems to be able to take the mess that we give Him and turn it into something beautiful.

Joseph was not only given a special coat by his parents but also a promise by God Himself through dreams. His eleven brothers would bow down to him and serve Him. That story is told in Genesis 37:3-36 (ESV):

Now Israel (Jacob) loved Joseph more than any other of his sons, because he was the son of his old age. And he made him a robe of many colors. But when his brothers saw that their father loved him more than all his brothers, they hated him and could not speak peacefully to him.

Now Joseph had a dream, and when he told it to his brothers they hated him even more. He said to them, "Hear this dream that I have dreamed: Behold, we were binding sheaves in the field, and behold, my sheaf arose and stood upright. And behold, your sheaves gathered around it and bowed down to my sheaf." His brothers said to him, "Are you indeed to reign over us? Or are you indeed to rule over us?" So they hated him even more for his dreams and for his words.

Then he dreamed another dream and told it to his brothers and said, "Behold, I have dreamed another dream. Behold, the sun, the moon, and eleven stars were bowing down to me." But when he told it to his father and to his brothers, his father rebuked him and said to him, "What is this dream that you have dreamed? Shall I and your mother and your brothers indeed come to bow ourselves to the ground before you?" And his brothers were jealous of him, but his father kept the saying in mind.

Verses 12-17 describe Jacob sending Joseph to visit his brothers in the fields to check on them, and the story continues:

They saw him from afar, and before he came near to them they conspired against him to kill him. They said to one another, "Here comes this dreamer. Come now, let us kill him and throw him into one of the pits. Then we will say that a fierce animal has devoured him, and we will see what will become of his dreams." But when Reuben heard it, he rescued him out of their hands, saying, "Let us not take his life." And Reuben said to them, "Shed no blood; throw him into this pit here in the wilderness, but do not lay a hand on him"—that he might rescue him out of their hand to restore him to his father. So when Joseph came to his brothers, they stripped him of his robe, the robe of many colors that he wore. And they took him and threw him into a pit. The pit was empty; there was no water in it.

Then they sat down to eat. And looking up they saw a caravan of Ishmaelites coming from Gilead, with their camels bearing gum, balm, and myrrh, on their way to carry it down to Egypt. Then Judah said to his brothers, "What profit is it if we kill our brother and conceal his blood? Come, let us sell him to the Ishmaelites, and let not our hand be upon him, for he is our brother, our own flesh." And his brothers listened to him. Then Midianite traders passed by. And they drew Joseph up and lifted him out of the pit, and sold him to the Ishmaelites for twenty shekels of silver. They took Joseph to Egypt.

When Reuben returned to the pit and saw that Joseph was not in the pit, he tore his clothes and returned to his brothers and said, "The boy is gone, and I, where shall I go?" Then they took Joseph's robe and slaughtered a goat and dipped the robe in the blood. And they sent the robe of many colors and brought it to their father and said, "This we have found; please identify whether it is your son's robe or not." And he identified it and said, "It is my son's robe. A fierce animal has devoured him. Joseph is without doubt torn to pieces." Then Jacob tore his garments and put sackcloth on his loins and mourned for his son many days. All his sons and all his daughters rose up to comfort him, but he refused to be comforted and said, "No, I shall go down to Sheol to my son, mourning."

Thus his father wept for him. Meanwhile the Midianites had sold him
in Egypt to Potiphar, an officer of Pharaoh, the captain of the guard.

Jacob believed his youngest son, Joseph, was dead! Judah, Joseph's brother, wasn't content in killing Joseph—he figured he should make a little money in the process. This is a picture of what Judas would do in betraying Jesus centuries later.

Joseph, of course, couldn't grasp the extent of his visions for the future. He didn't know all that they meant. We can possibly blame him for sharing his dream so vividly with his brothers, but we can't put too much blame on him. After all, he was young and had been treated differently by his parents ever since he had been born. These dreams he had aligned with the message he was getting from his parents: he was special. He was different.

Joseph received a promise from the Lord. He didn't know exactly how it would all look. And neither do we. When God gives us a promise, we only see in part. We never see the full picture. If we did, we wouldn't be required to have faith. Faith is believing in the picture God gives you of your future. Faith is saying "yes" to God when we don't have all the answers. Faith is saying, "God, I don't know, but I know *You* do." This is the same faith that Abraham needed to pack up all his belongings and move when the Lord said to him in his prayer time, "Go to the land I will show you" (Acts 7:3, NIV).

When God gives us a promise, He only gives us glimpses into the future—just enough to inspire us to move forward, yet not enough to limit our need for faith. Not knowing all that will come of God's promises creates an environment for us to trust, which develops our relationship with God. That's what God wants most—our hearts.

When God puts a promise in your heart, it's like a picture of your future. Sometimes, that picture seems impossible—illogical—based on your financial situation, background, or education. But we can't rule out what God wants to do based on what we think. We can't ignore the picture in our mind, the promise in our heart. If we do, we may be "in charge," but we aren't truly walking in faith.

If you're not in a place where you need a miracle from God, then maybe you should ask God to birth some bigger dreams in your heart—a promise!

|||||||||||||||||||||||||||||||||||||||||||||||||||||||||||||||||||||||||||||||||||||||||||||||||||||||||||||||||||||||

Maybe you're thinking too small and limiting what God wants to do in your life. Knowing you need a miracle tells me that you're dreaming with God, because when do, you'll always be dependent upon a miracle.

JOSEPH'S REALITY

When Joseph told his brothers the dream about them bowing down before him in the future, they weren't very happy about it. Their anger began to boil over. They simply had had enough of Joseph being the favorite! They suddenly attacked him and threw him into a cistern, an old, deep well with no water in it. Their anger and bitterness had totally driven them to the edge. Afterward, they began to eat their lunch and saw some Ishmaelites coming by. Judah, Joseph's half-brother, suggested, "Let's at least make some money off him!" They sold him, and he was taken to Egypt to Potiphar, the minister of defense.

Ironically, the enemy to whom Joseph was sold was the very descendant of Abraham and Hagar's child, Ishmael. Abraham's choice to run ahead of God caused so much heartache, yet God turned this situation around and used it for His glory. God has a unique ability in doing that!

Just like Joseph, we will have to face reality—problems that are out of our control, people whom we can't understand, promises yet to be fulfilled.

Joseph had three realities to face:

1) He was sold into slavery. He could blame God or choose to trust Him.

2) He was given a dream from God that involved others. There has to be a reason for the promise.

3) He was given a gift—a gift of dream interpretation. He could use it or choose to deny it and the God who gave it to him.

Eventually, Joseph was sent to Potiphar's house. Think of him as the VP. God's plan was beginning to unfold. The process was taking on its next phase.

JOSEPH'S OBSTACLES

The Lord was with Joseph so that he prospered and
lived in the house of his Egyptian master, Potiphar...
Potiphar entrusted everything he owned to Joseph.

—GENESIS 39:2-4

Even when Joseph was thrown into prison, he kept his good attitude. John Maxwell has said, "Your attitude determines your altitude." That's true in many cases. If Joseph would have sulked and moaned all day, there's no way Potiphar would have put up with it. Instead, Joseph did what he could with what he had. If he was given a task, he did it to the best of his ability. You and I can learn a valuable lesson here. When you're treated unfairly or simply don't get the job you wanted or the promotion you felt you deserved, you can sulk, moan, and complain, or you can have a great attitude and simply work hard with what you've got.

Joseph did just that. He served Potiphar 100 percent. Joseph knew that, by honoring Potiphar's authority, he was honoring God. Joseph knew that he didn't belong as a slave and that this was only temporary. He knew his true identity as his father's son. He was a descendent of Abraham too! He was an heir to the promise of God. God Himself had promised to bless their family, and Joseph held on to that promise within his heart.

Your beliefs determine your behavior which determines your future. If you'll choose to believe that God is good and knows what He's doing in your life, then you'll behave and act accordingly. You'll work hard, respect whoever is in authority over you, truly want the best for those around you, and love and serve whoever stands before you. God is watching, He will honor you in due time, and He place you where He wants you to serve. When you know that you're a child of God, highly favored, and that your steps are ordered by Him, you're content and at peace in every season. Your identity is secure.

Many leaders don't trust the process. They assume that what they want is what God wants. We cannot assume that our wants are God's will. Sometimes, God makes our desires align with His will; but even when we don't get what we want or see God do what we expect in the timeline that we expect, we can't assume God has forgotten us or is forgetting His promises to us. He is faithful throughout all generations. He works all things out for our good. He is perfect, and His ways are perfect.

I've been in pastoral ministry since 2005. Every now and then, people ask me if I think the trial they're facing is God's way of saying they're in sin. When we face an obstacle or trial, it doesn't mean that we're out of the will of God or "in sin." Obstacles can simply be a training ground—a point where God builds your faith and strengthens your trust. You're on earth with broken humans! Of course you're going to face obstacles and opposition!

If facing a trial or obstacle is an indicator of being out of God's will, then Jesus would've been out of God's will, because He faced many: stubborn disciples, accusing Pharisees, unbelieving people. In fact, the Holy Spirit led Him into the desert to be tested! We face trials of every kind that taunt us to give in and give up. But in those moments, we must remember that obstacles set by Satan can become opportunities for miracles! We must allow our faith to rise above the problems we face. We must face these obstacles with a good attitude and with kindness and patience for those involved. Sometimes, the obstacle before us is just another chance for God to show up and do what He does!

When Jesus was faced with empty wine jars, what did He do? He didn't assume he was in the wrong place at the wrong time. Quite the opposite! He declared that heaven would come to earth! When those who followed Him all day became hungry, what did He do? He didn't send them home; instead, He used that moment to turn the obstacle into an opportunity for a miracle. He empowered His disciples to take part and feed thousands miraculously!

OUR FIRST CHURCH PLANT

I remember God speaking to me about planting a second church campus for Rock of Grace. This is the church I had served at for fourteen years under my dad's leadership. I was in the process of becoming the lead pastor and suddenly felt God speaking to me about planting a campus in Cortland, the little town where I lived, which was twelve miles from our church in Kinsman. I did what most of us do when God gives us an idea like that—I gave Him all the reasons it wouldn't work:

> » Sharing a vision to multiply months after becoming their pastor isn't wise. I should wait a few years, right, Lord?
> » It will be hard to find a pastor for a new campus. You know that, right, God?
> » It will be hard to find a worship leader.
> » How on earth are we going to pay for that? What if no one gives finances toward this?
> » There aren't any good buildings in Cortland for that, Lord!
> » It's too close to Kinsman, our main campus.
> » What if I fail? What will people think of my leadership?

My list went on and on. But the more I prayed, the more I knew God wanted me to do this thing. I shared the vision, and in six months, our church of three hundred people had raised $250,000! God moved on hearts and gave people a passion to see our little town of Cortland, Ohio, come to know Jesus!

Many have become disciple makers! Many have come to Christ—even four of my neighbors have attended or still attend our Cortland campus! The obstacles that were piling up in my mind were not obstacles to God. They were opportunities for Him to show His power and leading.

Every problem is an opportunity for God to do a miracle! —Pastor Konan Stephens

|||||||||||||||||||||||||||||||||||||||||||||||||||||||||||||||||||||||||||||||||||||||||||||||||||||||||||||||||||

Joseph was given a dream—a promise. But like all promises, obstacles were soon to follow—problems outside of his control. What's most inspiring to me about Joseph's story is that he didn't complain and get bitter toward God or toward service. He had to be tempted, too! Yet he didn't get cynical toward people. He still did the right thing when given the chance, and he believed that God was still good and able to see Him through. He stayed focused on the person he was becoming, not just the position he was getting.

I am sure of this, that He who began a good work in you
will bring it to completion at the day of Jesus Christ.
—Philippians 1:6 (ESV)

God is not done with you! Are you frustrated with people you're working alongside? Are you ready to throw in the towel? Many other leaders have been there too. Some quit. Some believed the lies Satan whispered. Others held on to faith. And others chose to fight the good fight and hold on to promises spoken by the Lord over their lives. Many people are now following Jesus because they didn't quit.

Be encouraged: if you feel on the brink of quitting, don't. Don't quit leadership. Instead, quit "mastership." Quit believing that you are the master. You're not. Quit believing that the success of your organization is solely based on you. It's not. The *Lord* causes things and people to prosper. Quit "mastership." You don't need to control every outcome and every differing opinion. That's not leadership. Let Jesus be the Master. He's the only person for that job. Simply be the leader God made you to be. Let God, who began a good work in you, finish it! HE is the one at work, not you.

Don't confuse your role with God's. You are the steward. You are simply given the opportunity to steward well what you've been given—the people willing to follow you, the product(s) you create, the finances that follow. You are the steward, not the Master. Every time God has tapped the shoulder of a leader, He has given them something to steward; and in that stewardship will come obstacles and character tests.

Obstacles are those things on the outside that we can't control—circumstances that are frustrating. I'm using the term "character tests" for those things that attack our heart—the inside of us, those lies that Satan tempts us to believe—the enemy within, if you will. Here's the truth: after many victories over obstacles, the character test often follows. Like the reality stage where we question our ability to see the promise come to life, the character test stage has to do with our heart.

JOSEPH'S CHARACTER IS TESTED

Genesis 39:6-8 (NIV) says, "Now Joseph was well-built and handsome, and after a while his master's wife took notice of Joseph and said, 'Come to bed with me!' But he refused." When Potiphar's wife came on to Joseph, he didn't take the bait. He refused to sin. He said that her husband had been good to him and that he simply wouldn't compromise and have sex with her. His exact words were, "How . . . could I do such a wicked thing and sin against God?" (Genesis 39:9, NIV).

Joseph knew that his decisions either pleased God or didn't—that character matters. It's been said that character is who you are when nobody's watching. Although he could've possibly "gotten away with it," he knew that God would know. He knew who he was. He was Jewish. He was the great-grandson of Abraham! His family was given a promise! A blessing! He was a son of a royal line! He wasn't going to allow his circumstance to dictate his identity. He knew who he was before getting sold into slavery and ending up in Potiphar's house!

Many leaders today believe that what they do "on stage" is what matters most. They've elevated charisma over character, and that will be their downfall. They don't realize their identity first as a child of God, so they live from a place of performance or pleasure. If you live to perform—to impress others or to enjoy pleasure—you've forgotten who you are! Joseph was able to resist the temptation to sin because he knew who he was!

Do you know who you are—whose you are? Do you know the price that Jesus paid to make you His brother or sister, that God the Father calls you loved, special, and chosen? Do you know that God has promises for your future that Satan wants to steal?

Satan will tempt you to believe that your joy can come from what you don't have. True joy comes from knowing what God's already given you.

IIIIIIIIIIIIIIIIIIIIIIIIIIIIIIIIIIIIIIIIIIIIIIIIIIIIIIIIIIIIIIIIIIIIIIIIIIIIIIIIIIIIIIIIIIIIIIIIIIIIIIIIIIIIIIIIIIIIIIIIIIIIIIIII

When God's favor is on your life, even the world will notice and want you and pull at you. In these moments, you have to remember that you are on a mission. You are a leader, following Jesus and sent with the mission that Jesus has given you, whether that's in business or inside church walls. You are God's and sent by God to restore people to sonship, and you can't do that if you give into temptation.

Proverbs 22:1 says, "A good name is to be chosen rather than great riches, and favor is better than silver or gold." You can build a good name for decades and lose it in a moment. You are one decision away from ruining your reputation. What takes years to build takes moments to lose. God's Word tells us to be careful, to guard our hearts. God's Word even instructs us to run from sexual sin just like Joseph, to choose a good name, and to do the right thing.

Joseph wasn't led by feelings; he was led by truth. I'm concerned with how often I hear the words, "I just feel," among Christians lately. Do I believe God affects our emotions? Of course I do! I'm a musician and a songwriter! I'm one of the more emotional guys you're likely to meet. Yet I do not make my decisions based on my feelings, because I know that my feelings can lead me astray. I go to the Lord in prayer. I go to His Word. I ask Him to speak, and He is faithful to do just that.

There may have been a feeling of sexual frustration in Joseph. And Potiphar being was who he was, it's possible that Potiphar's wife was very attractive. It's possible that she teased him and made herself quite visible to him on occasion. Joseph was a young man full of testosterone. Let's be honest here. The Bible doesn't sugarcoat it, so neither should we.

We don't know the extent of Joseph's temptation, but we can't assume that it was easy to say "no." It's often hard to say "no" to lust, especially in today's culture, where pornography is becoming normal. Studies have shown that many men inside and outside the church struggle with pornography. Ministers fall into sexual sin every year. I recently read about yet another Christian leader falling into sexual sin. Why is it that men and women who are favored by the Lord suddenly believe the very lies from Satan that they preach against from their pulpits?

The Bible tells us in 1 Corinthians 6:18, "Run from sexual sin! Every other sin a person commits is outside the body, but the sexually immoral person sins against his own body." The Bible tells us that sexual sin *is* different—that no other sin affects the body like sexual sin does. What we don't realize is that, when we sin in our mind with porn, we are being coached into believing a lie—many lies. We are then one step closer to actual adultery. We also know Jesus said that, when we've done this in our mind and heart, it's as if we already have committed adultery.

Do most men have a strong desire for sex? Yes. But that doesn't excuse men from having self-control, decency, and integrity. God can and will keep you! God actually gives us a promise about temptation. He says in 1 Corinthians 10:13, "No temptation has seized you except what is common to man, and God will always provide a way out for you!" No matter what temptation you face, God will give you grace to enable you to avoid temptation and be holy unto Him. His grace enables us for every good work and righteous living. We cannot forget our identity as a child of God and a tabernacle of God's presence!

Do you not know that your bodies are members of Christ?
—1 CORINTHIANS 6:15 (NIV)

Think for a moment of when the Holy Spirit was given to the disciples in the upper room in Acts 1 and 2. A fire came above their head—each of them! Why? The pillar of fire rested above the tabernacle in the Old Testament as the people of God were in the wilderness. That fire represented God's glory, the light of all nations. It rested above the holy of holies. Now, fast forward to that upper room where the disciples were waiting in anticipation for what Jesus had promised them. The fire of God was resting above every single person, for every single person was now the tabernacle of God! God would be inhabiting them! This Holy Spirit is the Spirit of Jesus, and He calls us to be His holy tabernacle, free of sin. Do you know who you are? Knowing will help determine what you will or won't do. Knowing that you are God's, that you are set apart for God's glory, and that you are a leader in the kingdom God will give you the strength to run from sexual sin.

Our character is often tested when we have a degree of success; when we overcome an obstacle, when our idea has worked, when we're at a high in our life—that's often when Satan will come to us and tell us these lies:

» "You deserve more."
» "You deserve to get what you want sexually."
» "You have accomplished this, so you deserve what you want."

The lie begins with "you" when the truth is that it is GOD who gives you favor and appoints you to a position of leadership. It is GOD who has given you the great idea, the wisdom and grace to overcome every obstacle, and every good and perfect gift—including your spouse. The lie from the enemy is that you (apart from God) are so special that you deserve what Satan has to offer. That's the garden lie. The lie is that, despite the fact that God has given you everything you need to enjoy life, He is withholding something good from you. Satan wants to distort God's character. God is good—better than you and I will ever understand.

For Lucifer, the position of leadership wasn't enough. The jewels weren't enough. For Adam and Eve, the thousands of trees and shrubs bearing fruit weren't enough.

When we sin, we're believing the lie that what God has given us isn't enough. Something you need to embrace to pass character tests is the perspective of gratitude and genuine thanks. God has given you enough.

|||||||||||||||||||||||||||||||||||||||||||||||||||||||||||||||||||||||||||||||||||||||||||||||||||||||||||||||||||||||||

When you realize who you are, you realize what you've been given, and it's more than enough! You have everything you need to be happy and full of joy! His great love for you is amazing! His presence is amazing! He has given you all that you need for godly living and an abundant life full of joy and fulfillment, adventure, and friendship! Satan wants you to believe it isn't enough. When is the last time you were so shocked by God's grace towards you that you simply were overwhelmed with gratitude? If it's been a while, get back to that place.

When Joseph refused to have sex with Potiphar's wife, she lied about him, accusing him of raping her. She even tore his coat and took a piece of it as "evidence" when he refused to go to bed with her. She was angry for being turned down. She was likely even embarrassed. She had him thrown into prison. And Joseph found himself again in a pit.

Wait a minute! Joseph did the *right* thing and things got worse? Yes. Sometimes doing the right thing will get you into trouble, but you have to do the right thing because it's the right thing. Doing the right thing becomes nonnegotiable when you know you are your Father's child.

JOSEPH'S ENDURANCE

But while Joseph was there in prison, the Lord was with Him. He
showed him kindness and granted him favor in the eyes of the prison
warden. So the warden put Joseph in charge of all those held in prison
and he was made responsible for all that was done there. . . . The
Lord was with Joseph and gave him success in whatever he did.
—GENESIS 39:20-23

Joseph could've became so angry at God when he was thrown into a pit again, but he didn't. He could've said "God, I DIDN'T sleep with her, and You let me get thrown in prison!" But he didn't grow bitter towards God. He chose to see this obstacle as an opportunity to trust God and be true to himself. He knew his true identity and endured the lies, the pit, and the disappointment.

MATT AND THE GIBSON

I want to tell you about my friend, whom I'll call Matt. Matt walked into our church last year and, for some reason, the Holy Spirit highlighted him to me. I asked him to come forward. I didn't know why yet.

Three days earlier, I had purchased a 1950 Gibson 135. I had been keeping my eye out for this guitar for years and simply couldn't find it (or afford it), but I had wandered into a local store, and there it was. It was beat up, with small dents at the front, back, and sides. It had some serious belt buckle scratches, and yet it played like a dream! It was sixty-eight years old and sounded like the day it was made.

Three days later, the next Sunday morning while I was making coffee and getting ready for church, the Holy Spirit impressed on me, *Bring that 1950 Gibson to church.* I thought *No, I don't need that. I'm not playing guitar today. It could use new strings. . . . Nah.* For some reason, I could *not* get that thought out of my head, and I had *no* idea why. So I put the guitar in the back of my car and headed for church.

In the middle of the sermon, I noticed Matt standing near the back. I felt prompted to invite him up for prayer. I barely knew him. Over a decade earlier, he had married a childhood friend of mine, but I didn't know him or his story at all. However, God did! I felt that prophetic anointing come over me, and I started to share with him, "God is not done with you yet! Your character has been tested lately. You've been dropped, beat up, lied about, and accused. Yet, your character has been strong throughout this, and you have remained true," and the words flew out of my mouth when I said, "like this Gibson."

Little did I know that Gibson was his favorite guitar brand—I mean, this guy was a raving fan of Gibson guitars! With tears coming down his face, he was reminded that, though he was misunderstood, ridiculed, and judged unfairly, God His Father was proud of him for remaining faithful. I told him, "You've remained true to your sound. Your intonation has been perfect. Your attitude was humble and sweet. You are broken but not bitter. You were humbled but are not angry. Your character was formed more into the image of Christ. Like this old guitar, your value hasn't changed. It's only increased. Like this guitar, you've been beaten up but you still sound great!"

After church, we talked for hours. He told me his story of recently being lied about at his previous church. He told me about the strange ridicule and unfair treatment. He said, "I just felt so beat up and wondered if God still had a plan for me." Days later, a pastor called him and said, "God has put you on my heart for days now, and I feel I'm supposed to give my church leadership to you once I leave." Matt was stunned. Not only had God not forgotten about him, but also God was about to bless him and use him in a new way in a new season! Matt was disappointed and greatly hurt in his previous church experience, but he pressed on and trusted God. He listened to God's voice more intently than man's and, because of that, he didn't miss his next appointment.

FAITH > FRUSTRATION

A friend of mine, Bishop Robert Stearns, once said something that really resonated with me: "Don't let your disappointment become your dis—appointment." Meaning, you will have feelings of disappointment, frustrations because God didn't honor you or give you what you wanted or because people have grossly let you down. Don't let that cause you to miss the appointed time that God has for you to succeed in what HE has called you to do next!

If you allow your frustrations to overshadow your faith, you won't endure.

Endurance is the next phase in the process of a leader. If you let frustration beat out faith, you won't make it. Then you'll miss your appointment to serve God at a higher level. Some pastors quit the ministry after only a handful of years or quit the church where God sent them after only a few years of investment. Maybe their church didn't grow like they expected it to. They were disappointed in outcomes. They forgot that Christ—not people—builds His church.

Keep your head up! When you face frustrations, accusations, or simply feelings of regret from your own shortcomings or missed goals, don't focus on that! Focus on Jesus, the mission! Learn from what could've gone better, identify what you'll do different next time, and keep going.

**You either succeed or learn, but you never fail when
your aim is to obey the Lord and serve people.**

||||||||||||||||||||||||||||||||||||||||||||||||||||||||||||||||||||||||||||||||||||||||||||||||||||||||||||||||||||||||||||||||||||||||||||||

I'm here to tell you today that you *will* make it! You *will* endure and overcome feelings of inadequacy! You will be used by God in powerful ways! Your ministry is significant! If you're struggling with sin, you *will* overcome it in Jesus' name. Repent and let His grace renew you! If you're struggling with disappointment, you *will* overcome those feelings. God is not done with you yet! If you have team members who are lacking, you will be able to guide them and lead them with God's help! If you've simply lost your vision, go back to your prayer closet and stay there until God speaks to you!

"Faith is the evidence of things hoped for," Hebrews 11 tells us. I like to say it like this: Faith is knowing you don't know it all and believing the God who does. Faith is believing in Jesus, whom you can't see with your eyes but whom you can feel with your spirit. It is knowing that you're made for a better place—a place with no temptation to sin—and that God has made you and all people to experience a place with no cancer, no depression, and no fear! Faith is knowing that you were made for heaven and trusting Jesus to get you there as you step out into the unknown to obey Him, leading all who will follow you into the unique vision that He has given you. Faith is holding on to the promise of God over your life despite the obstacles, despite feeling inadequate in your talents, despite feeling unqualified when your character is tested. Faith says "Jesus is enough! Jesus is alive in me! Jesus is the answer, and I am not! Jesus can make all things possible!"

Faith is knowing you don't know it all and believing the God who does.

||||||||||||||||||||||||||||||||||||||||||||||||||||||||||||||||||||||||||||||||||||||||||||||||||||||||||||||||||||||||||||

JOSEPH'S SUCCESS

Joseph's gift for interpreting dreams never went away, and your gifts don't go away either. God ordained it that Pharaoh had two servants who were thrown into the same dungeon, shackled next to Joseph. They had dreams and he interpreted them correctly! He asked the one servant who was spared to remember him and mention him to Pharaoh so he could be given a chance to be set free. Genesis 40:23 (NLT) states, "Pharaoh's chief cup-bearer, however, forgot all about Joseph, never giving him another thought."

Joseph was not only thrown into a pit twice—he was also forgotten by people he helped! Ministry can be the same way. Leadership can be like this at times. There will be people you lead who simply forget you and how God used you to help them. There will be people whom you served the most, but who will treat you the worst. Choose, like Joseph, to succeed in the eyes of the Lord and hold true to your character.

Because he remained humble and didn't allow his heart to become hard, God gave him yet another chance to reveal his giftedness. After two more years in prison, Potiphar had some disturbing dreams and couldn't shake them. He saw seven skinny cows eat seven fat cows. Then, in his dreams, he saw seven thin, dying heads of grain devour seven healthy heads of grain. He knew this was a spiritual dream, yet he couldn't understand its meaning. He inquired of his magicians and servants, but they couldn't help. Then the cup-bearer remembered Joseph from two years ago. He remembered Joseph's gift and mentioned it to Pharaoh.

Pharaoh summoned Joseph. Genesis 41:15-41 (NLT) recounts their conversation:

> Then Pharaoh said to Joseph, "I had a dream last night, and no one here can tell me what it means. But I have heard that when you hear about a dream you can interpret it."
>
> "It is beyond my power to do this," Joseph replied. "But God can tell you what it means and set you at ease."
>
> So Pharaoh told Joseph his dream. . . .
>
> Joseph responded, "Both of Pharaoh's dreams mean the same thing. God is telling Pharaoh in advance what he is about to do. The seven healthy cows and the seven healthy heads of grain both represent seven years of prosperity. The seven thin, scrawny cows that came up later and the seven thin heads of grain, withered by the east wind, represent seven years of famine. . . . The next seven years will be a period of great prosperity throughout the land of Egypt. But afterward there will be seven years of famine so great that all the prosperity will be forgotten in Egypt. Famine will destroy the land. This famine will be so severe that even the memory of the good years will be erased. . . . Therefore, Pharaoh should find an intelligent and wise man and put him in charge of the entire land of Egypt. Then Pharaoh should appoint supervisors over the land and let them collect one-fifth of all the crops during the seven good years. . . . Store it away, and guard it so there will be food in the cities.

That way there will be enough to eat when the seven years of famine come to the land of Egypt. Otherwise this famine will destroy the land."

Pharaoh asked his officials, "Can we find anyone else like this man so obviously filled with the spirit of God?" Then Pharaoh said to Joseph, "Since God has revealed the meaning of the dreams to you, clearly no one else is as intelligent or wise as you are. You will be in charge of my court, and all my people will take orders from you. Only I, sitting on my throne, will have a rank higher than yours. . . . I hereby put you in charge of the entire land of Egypt."

Joseph literally saved the economy of Egypt! God quickly and miraculously elevated him to the highest position in the land, assigned to rule and reign as he wished at the right hand of Pharaoh himself. He was even given Pharaoh's ring, robe, and jewelry to indicate his royal position and power. He was beginning to experience success! However, this personal success didn't change the harsh reality of a famine sweeping the entire land, causing many to fear and some to die.

Joseph's father, Jacob, was also affected by this famine. He sent his sons—ten of them, anyway—down to Egypt to buy some food. When they got there, they bowed down to Joseph with their faces to the ground, just like in Joseph's dream. He recognized them, but he pretended to be a stranger and spoke harshly to them. He put them in custody for three days, accusing them of being spies. He simply didn't know what to do!

SONSHIP

When Joseph saw his brothers come to him begging for food, he was moved with compassion; but it's obvious that he was also moved with anger and bitterness. The emotions that raged in Joseph's heart in that moment had to be unspeakable. For a while, he didn't know whether he wanted to have them arrested and killed or if he wanted to hug them and forgive them. He wanted revenge, yet God was speaking to his heart, inviting him to want reconciliation more than revenge. He had the choice to be "right" or to be reconciled.

You and I will also have those choices as leaders. In times of turmoil or conflict within your team, you can choose to be "right" or to be reconciled, to take the high road by lowering yourself and being humble enough to admit where you were wrong. There will be times when you are right and someone on your team is wrong; but you can still treat them with honor by speaking with them about it in private. Give people dignity despite their mistakes. In doing so, you can cause your entire company, ministry, department, or whatever you lead to be blessed by learning about grace. Or you can allow bitterness to lock you in a personal prison.

Back to our story. The message was sent forth for Benjamin, Jacob's son, who had not made the trip to Egypt to appear before Joseph. Joseph had an internal battle: forgive his brothers and show compassion or get revenge. He remembered that, before becoming the prime minister, he was first a son of Jacob and was greatly loved. Joseph insisted his nine brothers go back home and get Benjamin. Joseph filled their bags with silver and grain and this blessing confused the men once they discovered it.

Jacob reluctantly let Benjamin join the brothers in their journey back to Egypt to get more food. When Joseph saw them coming, this time with Benjamin, he ordered servants to prepare a feast and invited his brothers. "The men were frightened when they were taken to his house. They thought, 'We were brought here because of the silver that was put back into our sacks the first time! He wants to attack us and enslave us!'" (Genesis 43:18). They felt they had been framed—framed for stealing! They were afraid for their lives!

When Joseph entered the dining room, the brothers bowed down before him, just as his dream had predicted. After seeing Benjamin, Joseph was overwhelmed with emotion and had to find another room to weep in, overcome with sadness for all that had happened yet so happy to see his brothers alive and well. Joseph choose to remember that, apart from being gifted and talented, he was greatly loved by his father and mother and had a family. Sonship was more important to him than success, and I pray that the same can be said of us.

Joseph allowed them to dine and eat as much as they wanted and then sent them home with as much food as they could carry. They again tried to pay for the food. He had a silver cup sneaked into the bag of Benjamin so that he could accuse them of theft on their way back to Canaan. They were brought back, accused, and Benjamin was made to stay. Benjamin, remember, was his only full brother. The other ten were half-brothers. Judah begged to take Benjamin's place and, in the turmoil of this moment, Joseph couldn't hold the secret any longer. He demanded every one of his attendants to leave so that it was just him and his brothers. He said, "I AM JOSEPH!"

His brothers couldn't even understand at first. They weren't used to seeing him in Egyptian attire and in that role. They had not seen him for years. Could this really be Joseph? Their brother! Alive! The prime minister of all of Egypt!

Joseph said, "Don't be angry with yourselves! Because it was to save lives that God sent me." Joseph understood in that moment that all the torment, the time in the dungeon, the false allegations of rape, the dreams interpreted, and the honor given to rule over Egypt . . . all of it was the plan of God to redeem and save everyone in the land. God was turning what was meant for evil into good. Joseph understood that God's ways are higher than his, that success wasn't the end goal, but being faithful to serve the family, redeeming mankind, saving others—THAT was the end goal and the plan of God. Your promise is always for the benefit of others.

Sonship is what our hearts must be after. As leaders, we can be deceived into thinking that other things are the endgame: wealth, position, power, or affluence. We can even think a certain quality of stage, sound, and lighting is the goal, but it's not! These things only serve as helpful tools used by a son to serve. "Success" in the eyes of people is not the final destination for a godly leader. Sonship is. It's where it all begins and it's where it all ends.

Joseph's life parallels the story of Jesus in so many ways. His story serves as a picture of who Jesus would be—what He would endure and accomplish for the saving of many lives. Jesus entered the world as the Son of God. Period. Yes, He knew He was on a mission to be our Savior, but first, he was God's Son. Yes, He was the fulfillment of prophecy, a miracle-worker, and a good teacher, but before all of that, He knew that His truest form of identity came in the form of sonship. He was the Son of God. This revelation and deeply-held understanding gave Him the ability to shed the false accusations of those who would aim to tear Him down. It gave Him the strength He needed to endure His followers leaving Him, deserting Him in His most difficult hours.

Jesus gave us His life on a cross to rescue mankind from its appointment with death. He endured as the "first of many," Hebrews 13 tells us. Like Joseph, He endured the pain of a friend's betrayal, the sorrow of the death of a friend when he lost his cousin John the Baptist, the accusations of His enemies, and the betrayal of His friends. God showed kindness to Him and was with Him through it all.

As the fog would settle in the early morning sunrise, you could find Jesus off in the distance, alone, praying to His Father. In those daily meetings with His Father, He was reminded of His identity—a son, a loved son. Just as Joseph knew how loved he was by his father, Jesus knew how loved He was by His Father. Just like Joseph was betrayed by his brothers, even sold for silver, so Jesus was betrayed by His brothers.

After Jesus was thrown into a "pit" by his brothers for three days, He remained faithful just like Joseph did. He was then quickly elevated to the highest position in the universe, seated at the right hand of God! He was given the name that is above every name. He took His rightful place, crowned with His new heavenly body and robed in majesty! Father God made all this possible by giving Jesus a dream, a promise that He would redeem mankind, become the firstborn among many new brothers and sisters and be Lord of all, and increase the family of God. That same dream must fill our hearts:

Giving thanks to the Father, who has qualified you to share in the inheritance of the saints in light. He has delivered us from the domain of darkness and transferred us to the kingdom of His beloved Son, in whom we have redemption, the forgiveness of sins. —*Colossians 1:12-14 (ESV)*

Joseph's story gives us a glimpse into what Jesus would experience and accomplish for us. Joseph went through the process of a leader, and God used him to redeem his brothers. Jesus went through the process, and God used Him to redeem all of mankind back to Father God. He is "the firstborn among many brothers." Our first joy must always be that Jesus is our brother! This proper perspective enables you to endure the process of a leader when you'll have to make some tough decisions that someone isn't going to like. They may even be an important person on your team. They may voice that opinion, yell, rant, and spew all kinds of poison about you. And in those moments, you can say like Joseph, "But God can. . . ." It's in the trials that God shapes our character and tests it. He removes the "I can" attitude of one who trusts in their own strength and replaces it with a "God can" attitude.

It's in the trials that God shapes our character and tests it. He removes the "I can" attitude and replaces it with a "God can" attitude.

|||||||||||||||||||||||||||||||||||||||||||||||||||||||||||||||||||||||||||||||||||||||||||||||||||||||||||||||

We won't lose all the ego that we need to lose until we face the obstacles, feel the betrayal, and get thrown into the pit. Before the pit, Joseph said, "I can interpret that for you." But after some time in the pit—after being broken, and after realizing that he is nothing without God and God's hand on His life—he responded differently. He responded with, "God can fix this." God can help you. God can do anything. Not "I" but "God."

God can work miracles! I'm just the messenger. I'm just the one telling you about an eternal God who is able to do more than you can ever ask, think, or imagine! I'm a son of God. I'm a child of the King, and I'll tell you about how awesome my King is and how awesome my Father God is, but what I won't do is tell you how awesome I am. I will only boast in the grace of God and His goodness!"

This subtle transformation of speech is an indicator of a major transformation of the heart—all because he experienced pain. One of my mentors, Pastor Ed Homer, likes to say, "I don't trust any minister without a limp." Joseph most certainly had a limp after his time in the pit. Joseph discovered the greatest thing a man can discover, and that's the satisfaction of sonship—but it was only after he'd been through the process.

Joseph prepared a new place for his father and brothers to live and enjoy abundance amidst a famine. This is a picture of what Jesus does for us in going to the Father to prepare a place for us to live in a new land called heaven, where there will be no lack whatsoever!

I want to reiterate that Joseph is a type of Christ. Jesus often said things like, "I only do what I see my Father doing. . . ." or, "I only say what I hear the Father is saying. . . ." Jesus knew that He was *first* a son, and then a brother, and then the Savior. The grace Joseph showed his brothers in that moment is remarkable, and it's a picture of the grace Jesus shows us. He forgives us for betraying Him and for being selfish. He provides for us all that we need. He prepares a place for us in His kingdom, living in His blessing!

Do you know who you are *first,* before your position or status? If you don't, you'll compare and complain, and you certainly won't reach your potential. Instead, let's allow the Holy Spirit to remind us that we are first and foremost loved by Father God! Let's live out our entire lives from that place—that place of sonship.

Let's allow the Holy Spirit to remind us that we are first and foremost loved by Father God! Let's live out our entire lives from that place—that place of sonship.

IIIIIIIIIIIIIIIIIIIIIIIIIIIIIIIIIIIIIIIIIIIIIIIIIIIIIIIIIIIIIIIIIIIIIIIIIIIIIIIIIIIIIIIIIIIIIIIIIIIIIIIIIIIIIIIIIIIIIIIIIIIIIIIIIIIIIIIIIIIIIIIIIIIIIIIII

Sonship is the ultimate joy of our lives! It's not a "goal" that we can achieve. It's an identity we receive, a gift from Jesus, our brother. God our Father gives us this gift. Jesus, the visible image of the invisible God, makes it possible. Rest in that goodness. Rest in that truth. Rest in sonship where there's no more striving, competition, pointing out other's faults, or shortcomings. Sonship. That's where it's at! That's what God, our *Father*, wants you to relish in and value most. From this place, we have a pure desire to see more join God's family. Notice I didn't say "a desire to see more join our church" or "our ministry" or "to grow my company." The pure, beautiful, and holy desire God wants to place in you is a desire to see more people come home to Father God and join the family, whether it's your ministry or not.

> *But to all who did receive Him, who believed in His name, He gave the right to become children of God.*
> —JOHN 1:12 (ESV)

When we let the Holy Spirit brand our hearts with gratitude for being the Father's child, our entire motive for being a leader changes. It changes into what God wants it to be. We now become motivated to see more people enter God's family. This may seem obvious, but really it's not. There's a trap that Satan wants us to step into, and that's the trap of building "our ministry" instead of God's kingdom. That trap we could simply call ambition. There's a difference between vision and ambition. Vision is what you believe God can do to better the lives of others—the preferred picture of your future and your city's future.

**Ambition is the personal drive to accomplish and conquer—
to attain power and prominence. Ambition is what you
think you can do alone for your benefit. Vision is what
you believe God can do through you to benefit others.**

IIIIIIIIIIIIIIIIIIIIIIIIIIIIIIIIIIIIIIIIIIIIIIIIIIIIIIIIIIIIIIIIIIIIIIIIIIIIIIIIIIIIIIIIIIIIIIIIIIIIIIIIIIIIIIIIIIIIIIII

Vision comes from a place of humility and prayer as God gives you this dream, this promise. It is usually connected to a conflict that God's Spirit has made increasingly clear to you. There's a problem your vision can solve.

Ambition comes from a place of arrogance and selfishness. It's that slimy, black sludge that pushes others down to get ahead. It will tempt you to stretch the truth to make yourself look more important than you are. It will tempt you to grapple for things that are not yet in God's timing or simply not for you. But like Jesus, you can resist those temptations with the Word of God and the trust that God's timing and ways are perfect.

Ambition will likely try to sneak into the heart of a leader like an unwanted thief from time to time. The second you see him intruding, kick him out with a confession of humility and thankfulness, a song of praise and a prayer. Take some time now to discuss how God is speaking to you through Joseph's story.

APPLY IT

Group Discussion Guide | P.R.O.C.E.S.S. | Week 2

Discuss in your groups the following questions:

» Is it possible Joseph was misunderstood by his brothers? In what way?

» What dream has God placed in your heart? Does it feel too big to ever come true? Are you too worried about being misunderstood?

» What does it mean when the dream is too big for you to accomplish in your own strength? And why would God put that kind of dream in your heart?

» Share about a "pit" that you endured or a time when your character was tested.

» Have you ever bought into the lies that came with success—that you deserved more than you were given? What do the Ten Commandments say about coveting, and how is that related to living a life thankful for what you do have?

» What's the difference between arrogance and confidence?

» Is it okay to be driven, to have ambition, or to have vision? What's the difference?

» Read John 14 and 15. What does it means to see Jesus as the vine—the center of it all?

Be sure to visit TheProcessOfALeader.com to view videos with your team. These videos will do three things: 1) Provide more details about the Bible stories for discussion. 2) Tell the stories briefly for anyone in your group who is behind in the reading; this gets everyone on the same page as to what you're learning. 3) Asks your group some good questions that will prompt you to apply the lesson and discuss it together. The videos are FREE.

A good place to start a prayer could be:

Father, help me to have vision without ambition, to advance Your kingdom and not my own. Give me the courage to never stall as a result of shortsightedness or fear. Search my heart and know my motives. Convict me if my motives ever change and my desire becomes selfish or self-seeking. Prone to wander, Lord, I feel it. Help me, Holy Spirit, and keep Your grace front and center in my life. Remind me daily, Holy Spirit, that it is You and You alone who gives me the grace to even breathe. Bring me to a place of humble thankfulness and give me a promise, a vision of the future where You can bring hope to others through my life!

Action Steps

I will remind myself today of the promise God placed in my heart.

I am sure of this, that He who began a good work in me will bring it to completion at the day of Jesus Christ.
—PHILIPPIANS 1:6

The promise God put in my heart is:

While this vision for your future may seem a bit blurry right now, keep pushing toward it. My next book, *Leverage Leadership*, will take you by the hand to help you establish a clear vision for your future and a plan to see it unfold.

CHAPTER 3

Gideon

> *When the angel of the LORD appeared to Gideon, he*
> *said, "The LORD is with you, mighty warrior."*
> —JUDGES 6:12 (NIV)

It was 2015, and my wife, Danielle, had just given birth to our fourth daughter, Eden. It was such a miracle. Every time we had another child, I marveled at the sheer miracle that birth is. I was always so impressed with my wife's ability to have this little human growing within her. It was equally impressive to see her give birth—and to survive that! Amazing!

About two months in, I noticed Danielle just wasn't herself. She was crying often, and was simply sad, and she couldn't explain why. Our family lovingly told her that she could be facing postpartum depression, but that was hard to swallow for both of us. After all, she was a rock! She was top of her class, and not only incredibly smart, but also one of the most mature, kind, and level-headed people in the world.

The depression only grew worse. I'd come home from church and she'd be curled up on the ground just crying. I didn't know what to do. I'd never felt so helpless in my life. Her depression was undoubtedly a spiritual battle as well. She asked me night after night, "Why would God send people to hell?" No matter how many times we'd talk and I'd remind her that God is holy, that God's holiness requires a heaven that is sinless and that Jesus came to remove all sin from all people so they could enter His heaven, she'd ask again. This idea of people being separated from God forever tarnished her view of a "good" God, and she was experiencing what most of us call a faith crisis. I personally believe that we all need at least one of those in our lives. A faith crisis pushes us to question everything we believe and causes us to come out on the other side knowing what we believe and why.

It just crushed me to see my bride in such pain. She couldn't sleep. She'd just cry for hours, and I simply couldn't console her. I'd remind her of all we have to be thankful for, but that only helped on occasion. Most nights, I was totally powerless to help her. Now *I* was getting mad at God. *Why won't You heal her? I know You can! Why won't You heal her? You said You would heal all our diseases! I've seen You heal people! Why are You withholding Your healing from her?*

My anger toward the Lord grew. My only response was to surrender that anger and sense of helplessness to God and admit, *Lord, You know what You're doing. You're taking her through something that's going to bring her closer to You. Give me strength.*

There were times I also had to fight feelings of anger toward Danielle. Is it okay if I'm honest here? There were times when I was changing the baby's diaper, feeding the kids, cleaning up, and wondering, *Why won't she just get off the couch and help me?* Then the Holy Spirit would remind me that she wasn't choosing to ignore her role as mom. She wasn't choosing any of this. She was suffering. She was in pain. She was hurting.

He would remind me in those moments that my first ministry was to my wife. I'd rub her feet every night and read some scriptures to her. I'd hold her hand and pray for her. She'd say with tears in her eyes, "Tell me this is going to end. Tell me that I won't be like this forever." I'd look her in the eyes and tell her, "You *will* get through this! We *will* get through this. This is *not* forever! God *is going* to heal you!"

Leader, if you are married, your first ministry is your spouse. Never buy into the lie that you should ignore the needs of your spouse "for God." Don't believe that it's just the price to pay for ministry. That is a toxic lie that needs to be broken in the church. For some reason, I find it a bit more pervasive in Pentecostal circles. It's not explicitly said, but it's implied on occasion. Your family is your first ministry. Don't ever forget that. If your spouse isn't okay, cancel the meeting. The other person can wait. Your spouse is first. Your children are second. Your ministry is third. You are not the Messiah. Jesus is.

Thinking that you have to be there—at every meeting—at every counseling appointment—at the helm of every decision—really has its root in pride. And trust me, I've done it. We all have. We're leaders after all. We're designed to solve problems. We all want to work hard, yet we sometimes are blind to the fact that if we are not taking time to Sabbath with our spouse and simply rest and *be* with them, then we are trusting in our own strength instead of God's. The more you trust in God's strength and ability to work in others and not your own, the more you'll delegate, the better you'll rest, and the stronger your marriage will be. And that trust in God's ability as opposed to yours is rooted in the truth of sonship. We must return to sonship.

You are not the Messiah. Jesus is. The more you trust in God's strength and ability to work in others and not your own, the more you'll delegate, the better you'll rest, and the stronger your marriage will be. And that trust in God's ability as opposed to yours is rooted in the truth of sonship.

I know how Gideon felt that day. Helpless. Hopeless. Exhausted from being beaten by the enemy day in, day out. Maybe you've been there. Maybe you're there right now. Let the Holy Spirit come to you right now and say to you, "Greetings, Mighty Warrior! You're going to get through this!"

A NATION IN DISTRESS

When Gideon came on the scene, the nation was in distress! They hadn't had a solid leader since Joshua. The Lord had always been faithful to raise up a leader to deliver His people in a way that invited them to repent and turn to God. It would be five centuries before King David would come on the scene. This was the time of the judges. There were some wild judges—namely Samson—and some amazing judges like Samuel. I think we might identify most with Gideon. I know I do. What you'll find in the story of Gideon is someone like you. Maybe, like Gideon, you don't believe in yourself or God's ability to do the miraculous through you.

Can you imagine having your food stolen—right out of your home—week after week after week? Can you imagine a neighboring nation or people group that simply has more manpower coming into your town and just taking what they want? Imagine how frustrating that would be! Imagine how helpless you'd feel! This is the moment in which Gideon and his family and their people found themselves.

The Midianites and the Amalekites had been oppressing the people of Israel for seven years! We may ask, "Why would God allow that?" Scripture says that the Lord let it continue because they had turned to false idols and stopped worshiping Him. Many Christians don't like that idea in their theology—that sometimes we are allowed to face the consequences of our poor decisions and sin. God allows us occasionally to experience the pain of our poor choices to help us see our great need for Him and His great grace for us. Gideon was in such a time in his life. He and his community were experiencing the painful result of ignoring God. As God often does, He spoke to someone to rise up and be the leader the nation needed.

GIDEON'S PROMISE

We pick up in Judges 6:11–24 (ESV):

Now the angel of the Lord came and sat under the terebinth at Ophrah, which belonged to Joash the Abiezrite, while his son Gideon was beating out wheat in the winepress to hide it from the Midianites. And the angel of the Lord appeared to him and said to him, "The Lord is with you, O mighty man of valor." And Gideon said to him, "Please, my lord, if the Lord is with us, why then has all this happened to us? And where are all his wonderful deeds that our fathers recounted to us, saying, 'Did not the Lord bring us up from Egypt?' but now the Lord has forsaken us and given us into the hand of Midian."

And the Lord turned to him and said, "Go in this might of yours and save Israel from the hand of Midian; do not I send you?" And he said to Him, "Please, Lord, how can I save Israel? Behold, my clan is the weakest in Manasseh, and I am the least in my father's house." And the Lord said to him, "But I will be with you, and you shall strike the Midianites as one man." And [Midian] said to him, "If now I have found favor in your eyes, then show me a sign that it is you who speak with me. Please do not depart from here until I come to you and bring out my present and set it before you." And he said, "I will stay till you return."

So Gideon went into his house and prepared a young goat and unleavened cakes from an ephah of flour. The meat he put in a basket, and the broth he put in a pot, and brought them to him under the terebinth and presented them. And the angel of God said to him, "Take the meat and the unleavened cakes, and put them on this rock, and pour the broth over them." And he did so. Then the angel of the Lord reached out the tip of the staff that was in his hand and touched the meat and the unleavened cakes. And fire sprang up from the rock and consumed the meat and the unleavened cakes. And the angel of the Lord vanished from his sight. Then Gideon perceived that he was the angel of the Lord.

And Gideon said, "Alas, O Lord God! For now I have seen the angel of the Lord face to face." But the Lord said to him, "Peace be to you. Do not fear; you shall not die." Then Gideon built an altar there to the Lord and called it, The Lord Is Peace. To this day it still stands at Ophrah, which belongs to the Abiezrites.

What a crazy God moment, huh? I don't know about you, but I've never made God a meal and then watched it be consumed by fire in front of my eyes! I have, however, made many meals and then stood in shock to see my meal and drink vanish into thin air. I now know that this is a result of having numerous children. At times, they are like high-speed rats. At the smell of food, they run to my meal and take it and leave as quickly as they came. I often picture the rapture happening something like the moment my kids take my food—like a thief in the night. I'm pretty much never able to stop them in time. Back to Gideon's story.

WHAT GOD SEES IN US

God sees something in Gideon that Gideon doesn't see in himself. God sees a PROMISE! That's not just for Gideon and "special people." It's also true of you. God sees your potential, your leadership gifts, and the abilities that *HE* gave you. He sees you in the promise of your future, not the pain of your present. He doesn't define you by your problems or your pain but by His promise. He doesn't define you by your lowly position. He calls you "Mighty Warrior!"

**He sees you in the promise of your future, not the
pain of your present. He doesn't define you by your
problems or your pain but by His promise.**

God has a way of seeing amazing things in store for our future that we simply can't see for ourselves. We're often blinded by the lens of our past. Like Gideon, we sometimes find our identity as a perpetual victim instead of believing God to be our victor and to change our circumstances. God first has to change our perspective. God does something interesting in this scene with Gideon. God convinces Gideon to change his mindset before God changes the circumstances. God wants to first deal with our heart, our fears, and our insecurities. He wants to see if we'll be honest and vulnerable with Him. Once He gets us to agree with truth—the way He sees us and the world around us—He asks if we will partner with Him to do the impossible.

**God wants to first deal with our heart, our fears, and
our insecurities. He wants to see if we'll be honest and
vulnerable with Him. Once He gets us to agree with
truth—the way He sees us and the world around us—He
asks if we will partner with Him to do the impossible.**

Often, our inner dialogue is so depressing that it becomes our outward declaration. We need to "wait upon the Lord," as King David said. We need to have encounters with Jesus so that the inner dialogue of our hearts becomes aligned with God's truth. Many leaders never change the world *around* them because they haven't allowed God to change the world *within* them. Their inner dialogue is full of fear and worry. Our beliefs determine our behavior. They always have and they always will. God first has to change our beliefs about who we are, who He is, and what is possible.

GIDEON'S REALITY

Before we face the obstacles, God first has to speak to us about how we view reality. He has to change our inner dialogue from one marked by fear to one marked by faith. But why even include us in the miracle? Why not send Gabriel to just wipe them out?

Couldn't God have just supernaturally taken out the Midianites by the power of His own hand? Of course. He could have sent one angel to do the job. But He didn't. Why? In God's grace, He loves to partner with His children to bring about societal change. It's like that moment when Jesus feeds fifteen thousand people with a few pieces of bread and a few fish. He could've done it alone, but He chose to work through His disciples. He chose to include them in the miracle. Why? Grace!

He begins by changing our view of ourselves.
He has to do this for us to believe the promise
He is giving can truly take place.

||||||||||||||||||||||||||||||||||||||||||||||||||||||||||||||||||||||||||||||||||||||||||||||||||||||||||||||||||||

He does this with Gideon when He finds him hiding in a hole in the ground! He redefines us. God sees us in the future! God has written all the days of our lives in His book, and He sees us standing victorious as a son or daughter of the King, not cowering down in a hole of fear!

Remember that scene in Narnia near the end when Aslan, who represents Jesus, gave Edmund a crown and a throne alongside his brother and sisters? In a stunning display of grace, Aslan saw Edmund not for his repeated mistakes but for his identity as being loved and affirmed by the King. Although Edmund was convinced by the White Witch to betray his siblings, Aslan (Jesus) forgave him and even gave him a nickname: Edmund the Just. Aslan could've let Edmund remain sulking in his shame, but he didn't. He called him out of it! God does this for us too!

I don't know about you, but I am so thankful that God doesn't define us by our worst moments. We live in a culture that likes to pile on the shame, even looking back years into people's history searching for ways to "cancel" them in efforts to bolster their own self-righteousness. We serve a God who says, "What sins? I forgave them all when you called upon My name and repented! You're free of all guilt. Your reputation is new! Your name is new! You're mine! You are a beloved, faultless child of God!"

Don't let Satan rob you of your courage by reminding you of your past. Satan's voice is the voice of shame; that's why He's called the Accuser! He accuses! Jesus stood in your place and forgave every mistake, every failure, every time you cowered in fear or even betrayed a brother or sister. Jesus forgives you! It's time for you to forgive yourself. Lift up your head! The glory of the Lord is upon you! Set your focus on what is to come and the promises of God you've yet to see fulfilled! God is faithful!

The feelings that you have today don't change your calling or your future. Your bad week or bad month does not affect the promise of God on your life. If God put a promise in you, the mistakes you've made don't cancel the promise. God is able to turn it all for good. If people have come against your promise and tried to stop you, today can be the start of a new season: a season where you believe God more than you believe man.

So how do we begin to change that inner dialogue and get it to align with truth? How do we get the mindset that God wants us to live in? It comes through prayer, and in prayer, God's Spirit will transform you! The Spirit of God is the voice of God on the earth. The Holy Spirit enables us to see the promises of God come to life! Jesus made this abundantly clear in John 14–17 as He spoke about the Holy Spirit helping us become all that He intends we become.

Don't forget, leader, that "It is by My Spirit," says the Lord in Zechariah 4:6. It's not because of your talent or skill, education or cultural background. It's the Lord who chose you and anointed you with His Spirit. It's His power working in you that makes you effective; it's nothing we can ever boast about or take credit for.

In the Old Testament, we see the Holy Spirit coming upon a person for a specific reason, for a unique role that they were called to fill. Scripture is clear that it's as if the Spirit came *upon* a leader when God was choosing them to accomplish His will. We see this with Samson, Gideon, David, and many others. It's not quite the same as when the Holy Spirit came upon believers and filled them with a permanent *indwelling*, like we see in Acts 2. In that moment, the Father sent the Holy Spirit to the apostles and all who were waiting in the upper room to *fill* them. It is, however, the same Holy Spirit, and it's the principle that is important to note. It is not you, your charisma, your talent, your good looks, or your intellect that allow you to be the leader you are. It's the Spirit of the Lord gracing you with His anointing! That's what we want. We want His blessing, His touch, His anointing to go do what He's called us to do. Paul often addressed the believers by first stating, "According to the grace given to me to be an apostle. . . ." He did this because he wanted Christians to be reminded that God's grace enables our work. Our works don't earn God's grace.

**God's grace enables our work. Our
work doesn't earn God's grace.**

IIIIIIIIIIIIIIIIIIIIIIIIIIIIIIIIIIIIIIIIIIIIIIIIIIIIIIIIIIIIIIIIIIIIIIIIIIIIIIIIIIIIIIIIIIIIIIIIIIIIIIIIIIIIIIII

THE SPIRIT OF THE LORD BRINGS UNITY

> *Now all the Midianites and the Amalekites and the people of the*
> *East came together, and they crossed the Jordan and encamped*
> *in the Valley of Jezreel. But the Spirit of the Lord clothed Gideon,*
> *and he sounded the trumpet, and the Abiezrites were called out to*
> *follow him. And he sent messengers throughout all Manasseh, and*
> *they too were called out to follow him. And he sent messengers to*
> *Asher, Zebulun, and Naphtali, and they went up to meet them.*
> —JUDGES 6:33–35 (ESV)

"The Spirit of the Lord clothed Gideon. . . ." There is a unifying call when someone is clothed with the Spirit of the Lord. I've been in hundreds of events in my time traveling as a Christian artist and worship leader. There is a notable difference when the leader on stage has been in prayer and is "clothed with the Holy Spirit." There is a sound, if you will. I want to humbly but frankly say that it is not the case with every Christian leader. There are leaders who are simply nice people, doing their thing in the church. Then there are those who, at the sound of their voice, seem to invite God into the conversation; at the sound of their message, they invite hearts to surrender to Jesus. There is a unifying tone in these leaders. They are leaders clothed with the Holy Spirit's power! That anointing is of utmost importance. The anointing that comes from time alone with the Anointed One, Jesus, is priceless and cannot come any other way. More than you need another podcast, book, or conference, you need the Spirit of the Lord to come upon you.

That anointing, that sound, like Gideon's trumpet, brings a unity like nothing else to those who hear it. Why? The chief role of the Holy Spirit is to be self-effacing and to point all attention to Jesus. This is also true of someone who is truly full of the Holy Spirit: they don't bring attention to themselves but to Jesus. This passion brings unity to any room they enter. Gideon was clothed from on high in order to accomplish his mission. Jesus was clothed from on high to accomplish His mission after His water baptism in Luke 4. You need to be clothed from on high in the Spirit of the Lord to fulfill your process. You cannot do what God's designed you to do in your own strength. Gideon heard the Lord redefine him, and he began to trust in God's ability to work in his life.

**The promise God's given you requires
the power of God's Spirit.**

THE SPIRIT OF THE LORD REMOVES FEAR

We all have fears. We're leaders, so we don't want to admit it. But sometimes, we're afraid of failure. Afraid our message won't be clear enough. Afraid our board or staff won't fully buy in to our vision. Sometimes, we fear what people will think, and that's natural; but it's time for supernatural!

Notice how God promises peace to Gideon in this initial encounter in Judges 6:23 (ESV): "Peace be to you. Do not fear. You will not die." God perceived Gideon's fear of death and drove that fear out with His love. Scripture says that God's perfect love removes all our fears. Do you have fears you need to give to God? I know I do.

Sometimes, I'm afraid of failing, of looking stupid, of messing things all up; and when I let that fear consume my mind, I stop in my tracks. I stop doing the very things God asked me to do. Fear is a trap, a hole in the ground. Fear will steal your peace and make you ineffective. Let God break off that fear by receiving the identity that He has given you. Like Gideon, you are a mighty warrior!

So, what happened with Danielle? Praise God, she was gradually healed from the insomnia and depression! It was late 2017 when we started to notice that she was sleeping again. The healing was not instant but gradual. I've heard from others that their healing also came this way. She'd tell me with gratitude in the morning, "I slept till 4 a.m.!" As if this were good news! I'd smile and say, "That's great, honey!" Remember, she couldn't sleep at all for months on end. She'd stare at the clock all night with burning eyes and a sad heart. But now, she was sleeping for 5 or 6 hours and starting to heal! Thank You, Jesus!

A big factor in her healing was support and prayer from close friends. We have some friends who somehow always knew when she was really struggling. They would call or text her and give her a scripture or a song to play. This encouragement was priceless! I remember one instance in particular when Danielle was crying on the couch and she said to me, "I just want Jesus to come look me in the eyes and say, 'I love you. You will get through this.'" I am not kidding when I say that, less than thirty seconds later, our friend Noelle knocked on the door! Without hesitation, she walked over to Danielle, knelt down on her knees, and said, "Danielle, look at me. I want you to pretend that I'm Jesus. I love you! I love you! I love you! You will get through this!"

I was hiding just around the corner, listening in, fighting back tears. In God's sovereignty, it was like it was only supposed to be her and Danielle in the room. Her and Jesus, if you will. I was honestly shocked at God's timing. I mean, think of it—how God had spoken to Noelle's heart maybe thirty minutes prior, how God knew that Danielle would say those words, and how Noelle would choose those words and even preface them with, "Look at me!"

God is *so* good!

God knows the pain you're in. God knows the questions that haunt your mind. God knows the fears you have. God will send people to debunk the lies that Satan tempts you to believe! God loves you more than words could ever express, and He has *not* forgotten you!

It was that summer of 2017 when I started to realize that Satan was hitting us as hard as he could because we were saying "yes" to becoming lead pastors at Rock of Grace. Satan knew what was coming! Satan knew that we were about to see a revival in our region and see many come to Christ! Satan knew that God was birthing in my heart a desire to plant churches and to make the impact of Rock of Grace exponential. Satan knew that we were about to see a spirit of adoption come over our people, and that many orphaned children in our region were going to find moms and dads in our church families! Satan wanted to tempt us to quit—and to be honest, I got pretty close.

What if we had given in and abandoned the promise God had given us to be spiritual dads to church planters? What about the lives that were destined to be changed—the marriages that were destined to be healed? What if we had quit on them and had thrown in the towel? What would have happened to the people we were assigned to impact? It's not so much that God needs you— it's more that He wants you to partner with Him to impact the hurting and lost around you. First, He has to deal with your heart.

Look at the impact of Gideon!

Judges 8:28 (ESV): "During Gideon's lifetime the land had peace for forty years." Forty years of peace—they were no longer being robbed and ridiculed! They enjoyed the fruit of their labor. They could end the day with a warm meal, watch the sunset, and drink a lemonade, knowing their hard work had not been wasted. Their kids were safe. Their lives were not in danger. Why? One man had an encounter with God and the courage to believe what God said to him. That led to an entire people living in peace and blessing instead of fear.

One man had an encounter with God and the courage to believe what God said to him. That led to an entire people living in peace and blessing instead of fear.

In forty years, what will be said about the city you live in because of your leadership? Who will benefit from your obedience? If success is less about stats and personal position and more about obedience and the opportunity to bless others, who will be blessed by your obedience to God? What will be said of "the land," the city, or the town you are in because *you* were there? If you're a pastor and your church disappeared, would the city even notice? Are you blessing them and involving yourself with their needs to such a degree that they would miss you if you packed up and left? If the answer to that is possibly "no," then maybe it's time to reevaluate what you're doing and how. It's time to get facedown in prayer and to ask God not only for a burden for your city but also a plan for how to reach it.

If you're a Christian businessman, how is the city you're in being blessed by your business and your Christian leadership? How are you bringing peace to your land? What "enemies" are being defeated?

IIIIIIIIIIIIIIIIIIIIIIIIIIIIIIIIIIIIIIIIIIIIIIIIIIIIIIIIIIIIIIIIIIIIIIIIIIIIIIIIIIIIIIIIIIIIIIIIIIIIIIIIIIIIIIIIIIIIIIIIIIIIIIII

If you're a Christian businessman, how is the city you're in being blessed by your business and your Christian leadership? How are you bringing peace to your land? What "enemies" are being defeated? What are you doing to defeat the lies of the enemy in the public square? Gideon demolished idols. Gideon went from wimp to warrior. Why? Did he attend a self-help seminar, grow up in a great home, or get suddenly blessed financially? Nope. I know! Did he watch enough TED talks? Nope. He came out victorious over these obstacles because of God's grace! God met him where he was and spoke to his heart. He came out victorious because he *believed* the word of the Lord! He believed the *promise* of God was true—that God would use him to deliver his people from the oppression of their enemy!

GIDEON'S OBSTACLES

He and his family were being overrun by power-crazed psychopaths! These ruthless, arrogant people became so sinful and selfish that they were stealing the food and supplies of neighboring towns and villages!

Imagine every single Monday you go to the bank and they tell you that the paycheck you deposited Friday was once again stolen. Imagine you're told that this is happening to thousands of people in every bank, and that there's nothing you can do about it. The banker smirks and says, "I'm sorry. The hackers have taken over. We can't do anything to help you."

Imagine how helpless you'd feel! That's how they felt! Their crops and their income were taken week after week by those bullies! Notice that Gideon's first response was to give up—to hide in fear. Your first response to the problem may have been wrong. Maybe you hid in fear. Maybe you've yet to even address it all. Your next response can be different! You don't have to stay in hiding! You can make a difference! It's possible that deep down, you know the problem you're facing, but it's simply so big that you haven't yet taken a moment to acknowledge it; you've accepted it as permanent. Don't let the pain become your normal. The kingdom of Jesus doesn't allow pain to become normalized.

You can stop the evil around you, speak up for truth, justice, and what's right, and take a stand against sin and lies. You can even stand for those who can't stand for themselves. There are people who are being oppressed or mistreated all around you. What are you doing to change that? There are children being trafficked daily. The United States is the number one consumer of human trafficking. Many of the victims are from countries where children and teens are left orphaned by parents who've died. What are you going to do about it? There are potentially homeless people in your city, and the statistics show that eighty percent of them are former foster kids. What could you do to care for them? Maybe that is your mission. Maybe that's the promise on your life.

If you're a parent, your kids have classmates who have parents in the middle of divorce. What are you going to do about it? You can pray, yes, but what else?

Maybe you need to be a part of a church plant closer to the school. Maybe there's already a thriving church, yet you haven't been involved in reaching those parents for Jesus. Only Jesus can teach a man how to serve his wife or teach a woman how to respect her husband. Only the Word of God gives us such clear advice on how to have a healthy marriage. You know that. You know that you have the tools. You know that you have the answer—Jesus. But what are you doing with Jesus?

Many Christians and even Christian leaders care only for the stage. Many of them never open their homes to lead a small group where they can share dinner with people and, ultimately, share Jesus. Part of facing the reality of your situation is coming to grips with the real struggles that people in your city are facing. I want to challenge you not to live in denial of the pain around you. If you're a manager or company owner, ask yourself, "Do I really know my employees?" Those you lead desire empathy from you more than to be impressed by you.

Those you lead want to know you're listening and that you truly care.

I would encourage you to have them over for dinner. Not once. Not twice. I'm not suggesting a one-time gesture or a box to check. I'm inviting you to let God do a genuine heart change in you. Don't rush this either. For forty days, the disciples experienced the resurrected Jesus appearing to them and teaching them. It took forty days for them to understand that Jesus' work was not a political takeover but an establishment of God's kingdom, which manifests itself through love. It took forty days for Moses on the mountain to be transformed into the man God wanted him to be. Forty is significant to God for some reason. It took forty years for the Israelites to wander in the desert before entering the Promised Land. Jesus was tempted in the desert for forty days right before starting His ministry. There's something transformative about forty days—or maybe, it's more like God is trying to teach us to wait on Him and let Him burn our hearts with His love. Let the Holy Spirit change you into someone who truly loves and cares for people. Don't think, *I'm leading an organization.* Instead think, *I'm leading people.* Don't think, *I'm leading a church.* Instead think, *I'm leading people.* Those people have real concerns, trials, dreams, and hopes.

I'm suggesting a commitment to a lifestyle change—a mentality change. I'm imploring you to open your home and do life with your team. I know you can't "do life" with everyone, but you can do it with a few. Christian leaders need to once again embrace the aim of discipleship and significance, and those only happen up close and personal. I once heard someone say, "Do for one what you wish you could do for all." That great line embodies the heart of significance and the heart of a leader who is starting to carry God's heart!

Do you know your team and see them as brothers and sisters? Do you know their heartaches, their stories, their pain, and their victories? Commit to leading them like Jesus would. Consider them family. Listen to them share over a good meal. Love them. Befriend them. Lead them by listening to them. One of the many great things I've learned from my parents is how to treat people like family. My dad often says during his prayer before a meal with guests, "Thank you for our friends, people who have become like family to us. . . ."

There's a lie in the area of leadership that I refuse to accept. It goes like this: "You can't get too close to your team. They need to see you as their boss, their leader, not their friend." I've actually been told that personally. I'm sorry, but Jesus debunked that idea quite clearly. He told His disciples, "I no longer call you servants, but friends." If Jesus can truly love and befriend those He led, we can too. Why? Jesus is our ultimate example of true, godly leadership. Does this open us up for hurt and betrayal? Yes, of course it does. You can only experience betrayal if you've truly loved. But did Jesus avoid betrayal and hurt by keeping his disciples at bay? Neither should we. If Jesus didn't keep His followers at a distance, neither should we.

GIDEON'S CHARACTER TEST

I asked my friend Will Collens to share his story with you, as I believe it's a great example of what God intends to do in all of us. After God gives us a promise, a calling, He allows our character to be developed in the midst of great heartache and obstacles; it's often in unwanted, painful circumstances that we develop the character of Christ—when our pride is crushed and our desire to serve others is raised.

I was born blind in my left eye, but I always had an eye. In the early 2000s, I was put into a position as a worship leader, basically because I was talented and my gifting as a leader was definitely seen; but I didn't understand what it meant to lead. So I "led worship." I sang songs; I definitely wanted to see a move of God. I grew up in the church and with an amazing Christian family, so I always "believed." But I don't really think I knew who I was in Him. My identity was that I was good at music and a good singer. I deeply cared for my friends, but for those I didn't naturally "click" with, I didn't really take the time to care. So, for several years, we did good music and saw no results. Melanie and Ryan were on that worship team. So was Ruth. Those of you who know my family now know that Martin and Ruth are family. But it wasn't always that way. I didn't like Ruth back then, and she knew it. I didn't treat her well. I gossiped about her. I disrespected her, even publicly. I sinned against her and others to whom I was called to minister.

Then, in 2009, I started to get severe headaches that really interrupted my everyday life. It got to the point that I would throw up every day at work. I ended up going to the hospital, and they found a mass behind my eye, pressing against nerves and my brain. Because I already had no sight in that eye, the safest way to remove the tumor was to remove my eye. Until the surgery happened, I was told there was a good possibility I had cancer. But I didn't. After my surgery, I wasn't allowed to do anything. No work. No music. No going upstairs. No holding my daughter. So my identity was taken away. I was a husband. I was a singer. I was a dad. I was a hard worker.

One night, I was feeling sorry for myself, and Tabitha put a Bible on the couch beside me. I was pretty upset with God, and I brushed the Bible onto the floor after she went up to bed. Later that night, I woke up, and the Bible looked like it was on fire. I picked it up, and it had opened to the book of Judges chapter 6—to the story of Gideon. I started to read. I was Gideon. I was afraid and didn't know my identity. The Bible says that Gideon was threshing wheat in a winepress, which is a hole in the ground. He was afraid. We see after God appears to him that Gideon actually argues. He says that God has chosen the wrong guy because he is weak—in fact, the weakest in his family.

But what I saw that day was verse 12 of Judges 6: "And the angel of the Lord appeared to him and said to him, 'The Lord is with you, mighty warrior.'" God saw Gideon as a complete warrior, courageous and ready for battle, even though his feelings were the exact opposite. It was me. God saw me as a warrior, and He sees you the same way. Something happened to me, and I started to worship God! I wanted to glorify and obey Him, and I knew what I needed to do, not because of some pressure or guilt but because I wanted to be nearer and nearer to Him.

So I told my wife, and the next week I showed up at church and talked to the worship team. I repented. I wept. I said we were going to glorify Jesus with our team and watch Him move. I asked Ruth to forgive me. The next week, I led worship again and, for the first time in my life, I saw someone be healed during worship. The week after, I led the first person in my life to Jesus. We built relationships and friendships in that ministry that are still strong today. We saw a revival. We saw many people know Jesus as Savior. Today, Ryan and Melanie are not only in ministry with me here but also at United Worship. Ruth and Martin are *literally our family. Do we agree on everything? No! But because God commands me to, and because I have invested more than a song in them, I know that even if I see another believer doing something I would not, I will think the best of them and be free!*

This might seem overly simple, but I don't think that the gospel is meant to be confusing. I think it is meant to be understood. I'm telling you today that if you see something different in me, or wonder where the anointing or fruit comes from, I can tell you with 100 percent confidence that it is because I know who I am, whose I am, and that disobedience is not an option. I am committed to being reconciled with my brothers and sisters.

Because of this, there is the commanded blessing! As a Christ follower, I don't get the luxury of going one day with something in my heart against my brother. Just ask the worship team or anyone with United Worship. Before we worship corporately or lead others, we surrender everything to Him, because there are lives at stake when it comes to how we worship. Again, it's not the song; it's the anointing that comes from unity—from a group that is reconciled to God and to each other. Please understand: I'm not saying that preparation or excellence isn't important. It is. We are called to do things with excellence as unto the Lord. What I am saying is that I would rather have the blessing of anointing than anything else, even the perfection of a program.

I would rather have the anointing and blessing of God over my family and life than anything. I don't want my own approval. I want God's approval. I want God to be happy with my character. I want God's blessing. And I want you to know that you can lay down your pride and reconcile with those you've wronged, that you can have the anointing and blessing of God over you and your family! It's not complicated. It's so simple. Reconcile first with Jesus. Get your heart in the right place. Make sure you're in leadership for the right reasons. Then, like the time

to reconcile with others, admitting where you were wrong, asking them
to forgive you.

The humility that Will is talking about brings unity, and that unity brings the blessing of God on your life! Don't you want that? Don't you want your life and leadership to honor God? Don't you want God to say "YES! I am so proud of you! You did the right thing, even though it was the hard thing"?

There's something I've told my kids many times over when they've just retaliated at their sister or let their emotions get the best of them: "Often, the right thing to do is the hard thing to do. God wants you to take a deep breath and forgive them, because Jesus forgives them and Jesus forgives you."

Back to our story. Gideon's encounter with *Yahweh* gave him a newfound courage to face the enemy. But he still had some pride and insecurity to deal with. Insecurity is something that needs killed daily. If you're going to grow in your leadership, insecurity is something you'll need to deal with on a regular basis. Insecurity causes you to worry too much about what people think of you and your leadership. Insecurity causes you to need the affirmation and approval of people you talk to. It pushes out love in a conversation, making you more concerned with your own reputation or ego than with simply loving and caring for the person in front of you. If we're honest, we're all insecure at times. Gideon was too.

Gideon did as the Lord commands, destroys the false idol of Baal, and burns up the Asherah pole. He obeyed God, but Judges 6:27 (NIV) says he did so "at night," because "he was afraid of his family and the townspeople."

Insecurity causes you to worry too much about what people think of you and your leadership. Insecurity causes you to need the affirmation and approval of people you talk to. It pushes out love in a conversation, making you more concerned with your own reputation or ego than with simply loving and caring for the person in front of you.

||||||||||||||||||||||||||||||||||||||||||||||||||||||||||||||||||||||||||||||||||||||||||||||||||||||||||||||||||||||||||||||||||

When you fear man more than you fear God, your character is in jeopardy. Early in your leadership, you'll be tempted to be afraid of what people think of your decisions. Even as you get older, you and I will still be tempted to make leadership decisions—or a lack thereof—out of fear: fear of what people will think. The more mature we become in Christ and the more we go through the process of a leader, the less fear of man we will have. Scripture is clear that being afraid of what people think is paralyzing. Living in fear of what the staff or board will think of your new vision will stop that vision in its tracks.

The fear of man lays a snare. But whoever trusts in the Lord is safe.
—PROVERBS 29:25 (ESV)

Over and over, Proverbs tell us that wisdom is the fear of the Lord. The "fear of the Lord" is a respect and reverence for Him—an understanding that He alone is God in heaven, and if He has given me an assignment and a promise, then I'd better pay attention and "fear" Him, respect Him, and know that I will one day stand before Him and give an account according to what He has given to me to do. The findings of that account will be the result of whether I lived in fear or in love. The fear of man will cause me to be afraid and ineffective. The fear of God will cause me to be committed to His direction and filled with His love! His Holy Spirit fills you and me with boldness and courage so we can be effective to build His kingdom, not our own. The fear of the Lord removes the fear of man.

I've experienced many occasions when God has tested my trust in Him. There have been many moments in which He has called me out of hiding in fear—out of the winepress and onto the battlefield.

I remember being afraid to share this vision of starting ten churches over the course of ten years. God had done the miraculous in making this assignment clear to me by using two friends who lived three hours apart, giving me the exact same prophetic word. As I prayed about the word, I knew what it meant—that our church, Rock of Grace, was to plant ten churches in ten cities in ten years.

You have to imagine how that felt to me at the time. At the time of my writing this, we are three years into this, and I'm much more confident now in what God will do. But while I was praying about this, I was incredibly fearful. Here's what crossed my mind:

» What if a church we start fails?
» What if we run out of money?
» What if I look like a total idiot?
» What if my church family in Kinsman feels abandoned as I take on this calling to spend a lot of time to raise up spiritual sons and plant churches?
» What if we fail somehow?

Then I remembered something I had preached just months before: my success *is* my obedience. My success is not the result of my obedience; my success, according to the Lord, is my obedience. It's my faithfulness to say "yes" to the Lord. Sure, it's up to me to make this planting network the best it can be. Yes, I should do it with 100 percent excellence. But I can't pretend that I am building this. I can't pretend it's on me to make ten churches healthy and successful. It's JESUS who is building HIS church, Scripture says! I can simply say "yes" to this wild vision and believe that God is faithful to His word! God said to my heart, *Just say "yes," and I will bring you the right people!*

After one year of starting our first campus in a town ten miles away, we received many financial gifts as God was moving on people's hearts, making it possible for us to not only pay off our first plant but also pay for a new building in Warren for our second plant with cash! God is *so* good! Many people in our church family caught the vision and gave sacrificially, and only heaven knows the impact of their generosity! This all took place in the middle of the COVID-19 pandemic!

When we face fear, our character is being tested. Character is formed when we're all alone—alone with our doubts, our fears, and insecurities. In those moments, we hear God's subtle whisper: "Stand up. Rise up, mighty warrior! I believe you can do this! Don't worry about what people think. Trust Me in this!" I have a better understanding now as to why the majority of angelic visitations begin with, "Don't fear."

Gideon's character was being formed by the Lord in this life-changing encounter. His first "obstacle" was the obstacle of pride within his heart. His pride said to him, "What if you fail in front of your family? What will they think? How will you look if this doesn't work out?" His pride said to him, "Don't risk it! You'll look like an idiot. They don't believe in you! It'll never work!"

The first obstacle we face is always within, not without. It's the obstacle of facing our reality and believing that God can work in and through us to change our reality.

I know you believe in God, but did you know that God believes in you? He believes you have what it takes to lead people out of the pain they are facing and into the freedom found in Jesus! If He didn't believe in you, He wouldn't have given you the promise!

GIDEON'S ENDURANCE

Gideon had to endure the opposing enemy and those within his nation who wanted everything to remain at the status quo. He had to endure people being upset with him for removing their idols. He had to have the courage to endure criticism from people who wanted to remain in their sin. He also had to have the courage to endure criticism from people who simply didn't like him rocking the boat!

Every time we step out in faith to do what the Lord has placed on our hearts, it's inevitable that we'll face some opposition and even be tempted to quit. God knows the pain you're in. God knows the questions that haunt your mind. God knows the fears you have. God will send people to give you truth—to debunk the lies that Satan tempts you to believe! The Father loves you more than words could ever express, and He has not forgotten you!

The question if have for you is simple: "WHO are you agreeing with?" This is the question of worship. Who are you agreeing with? Many times, we agree with Satan when God wants us to agree with Him. We agree with fear when God wants us to agree with love. We agree with worry when God wants us to agree with Him—trust Him, He tells us in Matthew 6. We agree with cynicism when God wants us to believe the best of others, and even of ourselves!

Who are you agreeing with? Gideon had a choice here. He could have agreed with the enemy and the rest of his family. They could have continued to be defeated, or they could choose to agree with the promise God was speaking to his heart—a promise of a brighter and better future.

This has everything to do with worship! Gideon made a rallying cry for his men to worship God. Why is worship so powerful? What happens when we worship? Why is it that when we lift our voice and sing—when we dance and clap, when we use our vocal cords to lift up praise to Jesus—something happens? Why is that? Jesus spoke the universe into existence and He teaches us that our voice and declarations matter!

When we worship, we are agreeing with the song of victory and the truth of heaven. We're coming into alignment with the song of heaven, whether we feel it or not. No wonder things on earth begin to change! When we worship, we agree with God about who He is. This is why worship and prayer go hand in hand. When Jesus taught us to pray, He said, "Our Father in heaven, holy is your name. Your kingdom come. Your will be done on earth as it is in heaven."

In other words, we need to agree with heaven regarding the situation we're in. In heaven, there is no battle, because Jesus has already been declared the victor! In heaven, there is no fear, because the love of God has already been revealed!

Let's go back to our story of Gideon found in Judges 7. God tells Gideon in so many words, "The army you have is too many. I want them to know that I am delivering you and that this isn't because of your strength or your leadership abilities." Notice how Gideon's army is trimmed from 32,000 to 300 in Judges 7:9-22 (ESV):

That same night the Lord said to him (Gideon), "Arise, go down against the camp, for I have given it into your hand. But if you are afraid to go down, go down to the camp with Purah your servant. And you shall hear what they say, and afterward your hands shall be strengthened to go down against the camp." Then he went down with Purah his servant to the outposts of the armed men who were in the camp. And the Midianites and the Amalekites and all the people of the East lay along the valley like locusts in abundance, and their camels were without number, as the sand that is on the seashore in abundance. When Gideon came, behold, a man was telling a dream to his comrade. And he said, "Behold, I dreamed a dream, and behold, a cake of barley bread tumbled into the camp of Midian and came to the tent and struck it so that it fell and turned it upside down, so that the tent lay flat." And his comrade answered, "*This is no other than the sword of Gideon the son of Joash, a man of Israel; God has given into his hand Midian and all the camp.*"

As soon as Gideon heard the telling of the dream and its interpretation, he worshiped. And he returned to the camp of Israel and said, "Arise, for the Lord has given the host of Midian into your hand." And he divided the 300 men into three companies and put trumpets into the hands of all of them and empty jars, with torches inside the jars. And he said to them, "Look at me, and do likewise. When I come to the outskirts of the camp, do as I do. When I blow the trumpet, I and all who are with me, then blow the trumpets also on every side of all the camp and shout, 'For the Lord and for Gideon.'"

So Gideon and the hundred men who were with him came to the outskirts of the camp at the beginning of the middle watch, when they had just set the watch. And they blew the trumpets and smashed the jars that were in their hands. Then the three companies blew the trumpets and broke the jars. They held in their left hands the torches, and in their right hands the trumpets to blow. And they cried out, "A sword for the Lord and for Gideon!" Every man stood in his place around the camp, and all the army ran. They cried out and fled. When they blew the 300 trumpets, the Lord set every man's sword against his comrade and against all the army."

Imagine that moment in the middle of the night. With only 300 men, they surrounded the enemy. Hands trembling, they tried to stay silent so as not to awaken the watchmen standing guard. Those men each were thinking about their wives, their children, their memories together. Were they about to die? Had their leader, Gideon, totally lost his mind? Were they being marched to their deaths? They could see their breath in the moonlight. It was cold. It was dark. Somewhere inside their heart was fear and worry—they wondered if these would be their final moments alive. But they let faith rise up within them—faith that drowned out the fear. They stood there in silence, waiting on Gideon's signal.

Suddenly, all at once, a roar was heard! A battle cry! They broke the clay pots! They blew the trumpets and they shouted God's praise! The enemy was so shocked and confused that they killed themselves! The soldiers had to stand there in total amazement!

Worship is agreeing with God—declaring who He is and what He's capable of. Gideon is not only a picture of us, he is a type of our Lord, Jesus. Jesus is the one among us—the human—the god-man who was hiding in plain sight. The god-man human who rose up in divine strength to deliver us and to give us victory! He did so with miracles! The enemy turned on itself. Satan thought that he won when Jesus died on that cross when, all along, Jesus' death was part of Father God's plan! The enemy's plans turned on themselves!

Leader, Satan's plans to destroy you will only be used by God to refine you for greater things! Your problems and battles only set you up to see God do a miracle! When God gives us a promise, like Gideon, He often uses people to confirm His word about our future. When Gideon went down to the enemy's camp and heard the dream the soldier had and what they thought about it, he was given new courage. A prophetic moment always does this: we're given courage to believe that the promise God spoke to our heart is real. Gideon does as the Lord commands and moves forward in faith!

He destroys the false idol of Baal and burns up the Asherah pole! He orchestrated an attack in the middle of the night, greatly outnumbered by the enemy. The word from the Lord had given him courage! Spiritual warfare is real. Heaven and hell are real. The supernatural is real. When you worship Jesus and lift up His name, you are agreeing with heaven, and that brings victory to battles on earth! As the leader of your organization, church or company, it's you who has to begin to align your heart and mind with truth and believe God for more.

Worship is spiritual warfare, and worship brings victory! Spiritual warfare in the heavenlies happens before warfare on earth. Leader, your prayer closet comes before your pulpit. Leader, your prayer closet comes before the presentation to the board of directors!

2 Corinthians 10:3-7 says this:

"For though we walk in the flesh, we are not waging war according to the flesh. For the weapons of our warfare are not of the flesh but have divine power to destroy strongholds. We destroy arguments and every lofty opinion raised against the knowledge of God, and take every thought captive to obey Christ, being ready to punish every disobedience, when your obedience is complete. Look at what is before your eyes. If anyone is confident that he is Christ's, let him remind himself that just as he is Christ's, so also are we."

Remind yourself of Christ's victory and let Him renew your mind. You and I are in a spiritual battle and, at times, we feel like we are losing. In those times, remember that worship is the key to victory. The weapons we have been given are not "carnal." They are not temporary or earthy.

Quit taking a knife to a gun fight. God has given you the Holy Spirit. God has given you discernment—it's a promise for every believer. God has given you the ministry of prayer. God has given you His Word. Take the problem you're facing before the Lord. Tear down Satan's strongholds in prayer and worship! How do we do that? We take every thought captive that doesn't honor Christ—even our own thoughts—and we repent of the disobedience in our life. If we need to forgive someone, we forgive and we ask God, "What is the truth in this matter? What is it you want me to know or learn in this?"

If we don't take our thoughts captive, our thoughts will take us captive. When Satan plants a thought in your mind that tells you that you'll always be in defeat, take that thought captive and remind yourself that Jesus has already won the victory. Remind yourself of truth and take that thought captive, submitting to the truth of Jesus and His work. When you do that, replacing the wrong thought with scripture, you are ensuring the thought won't take you captive. Leaders captivated by wrong thoughts are not only held captive, but sadly, their potential to lead others is now captive, too.

So what do you do when you're defeated in your mind? How do you get out of that pit? You begin to worship! Worship and prayer is agreeing with God. You can do that in singing. In dancing. In bowing. In meditation on His Word. In declaring His Word out loud. All this is worship; and when we worship, we're now in obedience to God's command. The ten commandments are given with a precedent: "I am the Lord your God who rescued you from Egypt." When we understand this revelation—that God rescued us—we are more apt to receive His command to worship Him and Him alone. Fixing our eyes on His ability to rescue puts in the correct perspective, the correct frame of mind: the mindset of victory! This mindset returns us to the Garden—the place where we rule and reign and have dominion. Jesus didn't only save you for heaven someday; He saved you to live in victory *now*!

Who are you agreeing with, Satan's view or God's view? Who are you agreeing with, Satan's perspective of yourself or God's? Who are you agreeing with, Satan or God? God had Gideon's army reduced to only 300 men. The odds were incredibly against them. God did this to prove that it was His power that would bring victory. He confused the enemy and caused them to kill each other! When you worship and correct your perspective, spiritual strongholds are destroyed and you're free to think clearly, believe bigger, and imagine more. He truly is able to do more than you can ever ask, think, or imagine! Do you believe it?

Let's think back to Joseph. He was tempted to give up on the promise while he waited in that dungeon day after day, night after night, feeling the heartbreak of being betrayed by his own brothers. Can you imagine his hands trapped in chains? Can you see him clenching his fists and gritting his teeth, thinking, *How could they do this to me? What were they thinking? I am their brother!* Maybe you've been there, too. Betrayal hurts, and it hurts deep. Betrayal can only happen, though, when one truly loves. Jesus truly loved those He led, so we know His betrayal cut deep, as well.

Like Joseph, I'm sure Gideon wanted to throw in the towel. Ask any great leader of the faith if they were ever tempted to quit, and they'll give you an emphatic, "Yes!"

Every now and then, I've asked ministers this question. It's a question that enables you to go deep with someone pretty quickly. It's like going full "Oprah" on them. Within five minutes of asking, "Have you ever been tempted to quit ministry leadership?" they'll tell you of a time when they were at their lowest. Have you ever been there? I mean low—like *really* low. I have.

I've had moments where my plans simply fell apart—when people I thought would be with me for life were now going to another city and, in their departure, accusing me of terrible, untrue things. In those moments, we can feel so beat up by the enemy. We can feel like a failure. We can wonder, like Gideon, like Joseph, *What happened? Why are they doing this?* We can be tempted to just give up. I've been there. Gideon was there. Maybe you're there right now. Why do these feelings come? They come because Satan wants you to give up on the promise within you and forfeit your future.

You have to understand something. Satan does not want you to fulfill the promise of God on your life! There is a very real spiritual battle taking place! There are people in your city who are waiting for your leadership!

||||||||||||||||||||||||||||||||||||||||||||||||||||||||||||||||||||||||||||||||||||||||||||||||||||||||||||||||||||||||

There are people in your city who need the hope of Jesus, and that hope is destined to come through you and the teams you raise up, not somebody who is a *better* leader. You believe in God, and now it's time for you to know that God believes in YOU!

SUCCESS

Let's continue our story with Gideon. Judges 8:16–25 (ESV) reads:

> And he took the elders of the city, and he took thorns of the wilderness
> and briers and with them taught the men of Succoth a lesson. And he
> broke down the tower of Penuel and killed the men of the city. Then he
> said to Zebah and Zalmunna, "Where are the men whom you killed at
> Tabor?" They answered, "As you are, so were they. Every one of them
> resembled the son of a king." And he said, "They were my brothers, the
> sons of my mother. As the Lord lives, if you had saved them alive, I would
> not kill you." So he said to Jether his firstborn, "Rise and kill them!" But
> the young man did not draw his sword, for he was afraid, because he
> was still a young man. Then Zebah and Zalmunna said, "Rise yourself
> and fall upon us, for as the man is, so is his strength." And Gideon arose
> and killed Zebah and Zalmunna, and he took the crescent ornaments
> that were on the necks of their camels. Then the men of Israel said to
> Gideon, "Rule over us, you and your son and your grandson also, for
> you have saved us from the hand of Midian." Gideon said to them, "I
> will not rule over you, and my son will not rule over you; the Lord will
> rule over you." And Gideon said to them, "Let me make a request of
> you: every one of you give me the earrings from his spoil." (For they had
> golden earrings, because they were Ishmaelites.) And they answered,
> "We will willingly give them."

Gideon was working with a people who were fragmented and far from
unity. Some of them were offended for not being called into battle, while others
were too fearful to fight. We find Gideon's diplomatic gifts on full display in his
response to the Ephraimites. He asked a few rhetorical questions of them. He
flattered them by complimenting their agriculture, and yet he gave the glory to
God for the victory over the Midianites.

Character tests will continue throughout your ministry, and perhaps most of them will take place when things are going great and you are becoming a "successful" Christian leader in the eyes of many around you.

One the motivations for this book was my sadness over the fall of so many Christian leaders. Ravi Zacharias, Mark Driscoll, Carl Lentz . . . they all, at some point, began to believe that they were the hope and the answer instead of Christ. The messaging is subtle at first. There's a lot of visioncasting and worry over brand, but then it progresses and becomes more overt. Sadly, many Christians can't discern it, so they stay because there is a longing deep within all of us to be a part of something bigger than ourselves. These leaders all have a way of painting that big picture that we can be a part of. The problem comes when they begin to make the message more about them than about Jesus. This causes them to keep the crowds and implies a sort of, "We got it right, and no other church does" attitude.

Christianity Today put out a great podcast called "The Rise and Fall of Mars Hill." In it, they share two clips in which Mark Driscoll of Mars Hill and Bill Hybels of Willow Creek both said the exact same thing at end of a passionate sermon. "Mars Hill is the hope of the world!" Driscoll declared. "Willow Creek is the hope of the world!" Hybels declared.

Now, it's becoming obvious. Congregants and outsiders started to take note and give warnings regarding the insulated, arrogant mindset of these leaders and the culture within their church leadership. The CT podcast host attempted to explain "what happened" with Christian leaders like Mark Driscoll.

The pastor's vision makes it clear that, if you're on board with the church, then you're on a mission from God. Add to that the love of celebrity and the weight of authority we give to celebrities by sheer virtue of the fact that they're famous, and you can see how success in ministry creates a virtuous cycle. You convey authority by communicating a vision, and then success has a way of confirming that authority, further establishing it, and expanding it.

Then growth leads to growth, and that growth leads to higher and higher platforms—greater celebrity for the leader—which in turn strengthens his or her authority. At the heart of this is charisma, the ability to compellingly communicate that vision and, over the years, to steward the story of the church in relation to that vision. What's missing, of course, is the need for actual spiritual authority. In other words, character and the resulting potential for imbalance—where the ability to communicate vision and captivate a crowd vastly eclipses one's integrity—sets the table for the kinds of spiritual disasters we see when pastors on global platforms like Mars Hill ultimately fall. Maybe we shouldn't call it a virtuous cycle. Maybe it's a vicious cycle.

Leadership Network had done some experimenting in bringing together younger leaders into the fold to learn from them so as not insulate themselves by only having ideas around Christian leadership based on guys of their age. They didn't want tunnel vision. The motivation to include Driscoll, I think, was warranted; I believe, as does the host of the podcast, that their posture was one of humility—a belief that "we can learn from someone who is in their sixties and from someone in their twenties and thirties." The problem is that, when abusive pastors like Driscoll are given more platform, it often makes matters worse; as their ego grows, so does their audacious abuse—abuse of the pulpit and of those they lead.

Mark's condescending and polarizing speeches became more vulgar and even more sexual in nature as time went on, and very few had the courage to confront him. When someone did, they were hit by "the bus." Two elders were asked to read through the bylaws and make some suggestions. They simply were doing their job and brought those suggestions to Pastor Mark. Mark fired them in between services on Sunday morning, as he felt they were stopping him from moving forward. He was the guest speaker at a conference soon after, where his "famous last words" were captured:

> *I'd like to go full Old Testament on some guys if I wouldn't end up on CNN for it. Some gotta get run over by the bus. There's a pile of dead bodies behind the Mars Hill bus, and by God's grace, it'll be a mountain before we're done. You either get on the bus, out of the way of the bus, or run over by the bus. It's that simple.*

Ministers like this are hard to understand. How did it get that bad? How did they continue? There are many reasons, but one obvious reason is that people in the pews and people who backed him and booked him valued charisma over character. They knew that, if they booked him, there would be more clicks, more butts in the seats, more tickets sold, and the list goes on. This problem of valuing charisma over character is our problem. It's all of us who've booked that speaker, ignored the voice of the Holy Spirit, and been too afraid to ask the hard questions.

I would argue that character can only be known with time. I want to remind you that God wants to grow your character and make you more like Jesus now and tomorrow and the rest of your life. Leadership in the kingdom isn't something you arrive at. It's a journey—a journey of leading and learning—learning to be more like your brother Jesus.

Part of having character is valuing your elders, even if you are seen as successful. It's acknowledging their work and their sacrifices that enable you to be where you are. You are not in a position of leadership because you're all that and a bag of chips. You're in a position of leadership because someone, likely many someones, paved the way for you before you were even born. They started the church, took a second mortgage on their home, and risked everything. They built the stage you're standing on. They started the college you attended. They built the company you now lead in. Don't miss this important perspective.

**Make the choice to continually honor leaders who
have paved the way for you to be where you are. In
doing so, you choose character over charisma. You
choose sonship over success. You choose Jesus
over Babylon. A leader who has embraced sonship
values the spiritual fathers who've gone before.**

||||||||||||||||||||||||||||||||||||||||||||||||||||||||||||||||||||||||||||||||||||||||||||||||||||||||||||||||||||||||||||

SONSHIP

I noticed two peculiar lines when I read this passage in chapter 8. The first line is when they answered Gideon, "As you are, so were they. Every one of them resembled the son of a king."

It's interesting that Gideon's view of himself was initially quite low. He was hiding. He was afraid of the enemy. He was filled with anxiety. He was not confident *until* he had an encounter with the Lord. Once he encountered God, received a promise, and believed in that promise, his whole life changed. Other people even noticed the difference in Gideon. They said he "resembled the son of a king." His disposition changed. His attitude changed. The son of a king would be walking with his head held high, in confidence. A king's son knows who he is and acts differently than everyone else. He's a prince, an heir to the throne. His identity is established. He isn't insecure. He *is* secure. He knows who he is. He isn't afraid. He isn't trying to prove anything. He simply is who he is: the son of a king. He's not arrogant. He's confident.

Insecure leaders feel the need to voice their accomplishments to impress you. This comes from a fear of not being respected. Christian leaders who are secure in their sonship and calling are different. They've had an encounter with the Lord. They don't feel the need to prove anything or impress anyone. They simply aim to love the person in front of them and be a good steward of their assignments. Gideon's life changed after that encounter with God. He now "resembled the son of a king." You are one encounter away from an entirely different life.

You are one encounter away from an entirely different life.

IIIIIIIIIIIIIIIIIIIIIIIIIIIIIIIIIIIIIIIIIIIIIIIIIIIIIIIIIIIIIIIIIIIIIIIIIIIIIIIIIIIIIIIIIIIIIIIIIIIIIIIIIIIIIIIIIIIIIIIIIIIIIIIIIII

One encounter with God can change the trajectory of your life. I've seen this over and over. I've seen addicts encounter the presence of Jesus and the power of His Spirit and be changed in an instant. I've seen them turn from living with a victim mindset to an overcomer mindset. I've seen men and women become completely new people after an encounter with God.

Christian leaders or those who are called to be leaders can make one of two mistakes. First, they never begin. They believe they are a victim and will always be one. They don't believe they can "do anything" for God. They are hiding in the winepress, afraid. They lack confidence and courage. They simply don't believe that God can help them, and they certainly don't believe God can help others *through* them. Maybe that's you. Today, that changes! Let God's Holy Spirit convict you of that false pride and fear of man. Let God forgive you for believing the enemy's accusation instead of the Father's declaration.

The second mistake is another type of insecurity. It is seen in the leader who feels the need to impress people with his or her achievements. They're arrogant, proud, and usually make the worst listeners. Either one of these mistakes is a trap of insecurity; it's a character thing. It's frankly something that God needs to deal with in our hearts.

Gideon was in that first group. He felt he would always be a victim. After all, he was getting used to it. Satan wants you to normalize your pain. Jesus wants you to look upon His face and be transformed!

1 Corinthians 3:18 says that we become like Jesus as we behold Him! As we look into the eyes of Jesus, we go from glory to glory and are transformed! I

think there are far too many leaders in our businesses and pastors in our pulpits who are operating in their own strength, unaware that God wants to encounter them, embolden them, and fill them with His Spirit! Can you imagine if every Christian leader and minister encountered God like Gideon did that day? Insecurity is driven out of the heart by encounters with Jesus! Remember, you are one encounter away from an entirely different life.

Let me help you picture what's it like for someone who's fallen into that second trap of insecurity. I remember attending a gathering of ministers a few years ago where I had two very different experiences with the two people joining me onstage that night. It is always such a blessing to get together with other ministers in any sort of event that brings unity to God's kingdom. I love those kinds of events! The vast majority of ministers I've met over the years have been incredibly Christ-like and kind.

However, I want to describe the difference between the two pastors I met that night to illustrate this virus of insecurity. The first pastor I met—we'll call him Tim—was telling me about what God had been teaching him lately. Tim asked me a lot of questions. He asked me about my family and seemed genuinely interested in my responses. Tim was humbled to be a part of the event. It was a joy to get to know him.

The second guy I met was the other singer—we'll and call him Mark. I'm just going to say it like it is—Mark was almost repulsive! I'll never forget it. From the first second I shook his hand, he started telling me about his accomplishments. I remember thinking it was odd, because I hadn't asked. Mark went on and on, describing to me the famous artists he has been on stage with, the number of people who have attended his events, and the number of CDs he has sold. He didn't look me in the eye much. I remember that. It was about ten minutes of just a water hose of Mark describing to me the Mark Show at the Mark Awards. I have a feeling the Mark Awards were not held annually but daily for this guy. I remember at some point just bowing out of the conversation and going over to tune my guitar, and I remember thinking about the stark difference between Tim and Mark.

Tim was humble, kind, Christ-like, and a good listener. I'd share, then ask him a question and he'd share. We genuinely got to know one another and enjoyed it. Mark was trying to prove himself to me, doing his very best to impress me. I remember thinking, *Wow. What a difference between those two. Lord, make me like Tim.*

Now, maybe you are more discreet than Mark, but it's possible you've done that too; we all have. At times, we feel the need to let people know how important we are. What is that called? Insecurity! Pride! If you catch yourself in that moment, let the Holy Spirit stop you. Let Him speak to your heart and simply cause you to ask questions and listen.

**When you value sonship, you value other sons;
and you can't lead those you don't value.**

When you value being a "ruler," you value "ruling"; therefore, you really only value yourself. God is raising up leaders across the globe who care more about those they lead than they care about themselves. God is raising up Christ-like leaders who understand that to lead means to serve.

The other line I wanted to point out to you from this passage is verse 23: "Gideon said to them, 'I will not rule over you, and my son will not rule over you; the LORD will rule over you.'" Do you remember what we learned in the life of Joseph? It wasn't until he was in the pit for years that he changed the way he responded to the request for his dream interpretation skills ever so slightly. Initially, he said, "Yes, I can interpret dreams." After years in prison, with no ego left, he began to respond, "I cannot interpret dreams, but God can, and I will tell you what He says."

After an encounter with the Lord, you humbly see yourself as one of many—a child of God with many brothers and sisters. You don't feel the need to "rule over" anyone. Think of it this way: it's like you know that, as a parent, Father God has whispered in your ear, "You are special to Me! You're my favorite." Now that you're older, you realize that He's told every child that! It doesn't diminish its truth, though. You really are special, and so is everyone else.

When you go through the process of a leader and let the character of Christ be formed in you, you won't feel the need to appear more important than anyone. Christian leadership isn't about ruling over anyone. It's about serving people.

It isn't about looking important; it's about making others know how important *they are* to King Jesus. It's about wanting them to trust God as their King, their Lord, and their ruler. Our goal as Christian leaders is not to make people like us, but to make them like Jesus—not to make them fans of ours, but fans of Jesus. Our goal is not to hope they love us but to hope they love Jesus. May we shine a light on Jesus so bright that they see Him, are changed by Him, and love Him all the days of their lives!

According to Ephesians 4, God's desire is that we become like Jesus, His Son. That is His primary goal in our livevs. The Father wants us to know Jesus, to love Him, and to become like Him. We do that through daily surrender to His plan and His ways, through encouraging one another by using our giftings, and through simply aiming at sonship. Our highest calling and greatest joy is to have Jesus as our brother and to become more like Him. The same Holy Spirit that filled Jesus can fill us and cause us to also do the will of our Father, hearing what He hears and seeing what He sees!

This is a question of identity. Do you see yourself as a son before you see yourself as a leader, a "boss"? You need to. If you don't, you'll fall into the trap of needing to be liked and wanting to "rule over" instead of serve.

I want to briefly tell you about my sister and brother-in-law. Jim and Jessie had a dream, a promise in their heart, to one day own their own flooring business. God made that dream a reality, and now they take their ministry experience and love for Jesus into their workplace week after week. They noticed that one of their staff wasn't herself. They took the time to ask what was wrong. In that display of empathy, they learned she was behind on some bills. They reached out to me to see if our church could work with them in a way that each of us could pitch in and provide a nice financial blessing to her. She was ecstatic to get that blessing. We believe her heart is more open now than ever to receive the gospel and God's love.

A Christian leader who hasn't allowed Christ to be formed in their heart through adversity and obstacles won't take the time to ask their employee, "What's wrong? How can I help? Can I pray with you? Are you *really* okay?" These type of leaders are rare. They've gone through the process. They've let the Holy Spirit prune them and remove the need to rule, replacing it with a desire to serve. It's beautiful! It's God's kingdom on full display!

SONS VALUE FAMILY

Sons value family. Rulers don't. Again, are you a son or a ruler? Maybe you're a CEO or COO. Maybe you're the president of a company or a chairman of the board. Maybe you're the senior pastor. While that may be your title, first, you're a child of God. That must be your identity. Identity must precede an assignment and come before a title. A title is given during an assignment. Assignments will come and go with seasons, but your identity remains. If you define your identity by your role, assignment, or title, you will find yourself at a great loss when that title is taken away from you. When you define your identity by your sonship—when you put your joy *exclusively* in the fact that Jesus is your brother and Savior and God is your Father—then you will have true joy no matter what! Then you will know who you are whether you are succeeding in your role or even if you find yourself without one. When seasons change, identity remains.

God wants a full house! Colossians 1 tells us that Jesus came to bring many more sons and daughters into God's family! He came to qualify us to share in His inheritance!

Because Gideon didn't see himself as a son, a child of God, he didn't see the need to have spiritual sons. Sadly, like many leaders in today's world, Gideon didn't raise spiritual sons. While God used Gideon in a powerful way and we celebrate that, I am heartbroken over one tiny verse at the end of Gideon's story. It comes from Judges 8:33 (NIV): "No sooner had Gideon died than the Israelites again prostituted themselves to the Baals [false gods]."

Wow! So God used Gideon to defeat the enemy. Gideon and God's people lived in a state of peace and blessings for four decades. Then, the minute Gideon passed away, there was a leadership vacuum. People did what they saw fit and turned from trusting in God. The question then is this: "Why didn't Gideon raise up a leader, a spiritual son, to take his place?"

There are many possible answers to that question. Here's one: it's hard. Being a pastor or a leader, people are constantly needing your ear. You find fulfillment in helping people and solving problems. Your schedule is full! Maybe you're like me, and you've got children who come first in your life. They should. But what if you and I made it a priority to raise *spiritual* sons and daughters? What if we asked the Lord to give us a spiritual heritage by sending us a few people to mentor? What if we met with them every single week—or, at the very least, once a month—to pour into them, listen to them, read scripture with them, and pray for them? Why is it so rare to see this in today's Christian landscape?

Today's culture is no different from that of the Israeli people three centuries ago. Town to town across America, you can find heroes of the faith preaching the truth of God's Word week after week. Yet so few are asking the Lord, "Who's next? Whom should I mentor to take my place when I get older? To whom can I pass my mantle and my blessing?"

In city after city, you'll find Christian businessmen who are trying to build a business, trying to "do it all," never learning the power of delegation and authority—the power of the team. Sadly, when they die, their company dies with them. When the company dies, opportunities die—opportunities for employment, a chance for a man or woman to provide for their families and have the dignity that comes with hard work and the contribution of your gifts and talents; opportunities for Christian witness in the public square and opportunities for kingdom building die with the death of the leader that doesn't delegate. Why? They were leading with a nearsighted view. The Holy Spirit wants to make you a farsighted leader. He will help you not only conduct business but lead leaders and even father sons and daughters.

In city after city, you'll find pastors who are truly doing an amazing job at pastoring. There is no doubt that their sermons cause people to put their faith in Jesus. No doubt, when they speak with someone in their office, that person knows they are loved and cared for. However, if that pastor suddenly develops cancer, there's often a sense of, "Who can step in to lead us if we lose our pastor?" With no one in sight, the church feels incredibly lost—just like the people of Israel when Gideon died. The church may struggle for months searching for people to fill the pulpit and lead the teams, but slowly, it dies as members give up. Sadly, this is the story of thousands of churches every year. Why? The leader was nearsighted and didn't raise up spiritual sons and daughters, people who could take the leadership mantle at some point in the future.

My parents, Mark and Pam, pastored Rock of Grace for twenty-six years, leading hundreds of people to Jesus. Over the last five years of his time as senior pastor, my dad asked me if I were interested in the role. I'd always responded with this: "I am so satisfied in my season of life right now that I'd really have to hear the Lord speak to me if He wants me to become the pastor. I know He'll speak to me about it if He wants that to happen." That was my response from

2010 until early 2015. Suddenly, God's Spirit kept prompting me to think about becoming the pastor. I'd pray about it and, although I had so many doubts about my ability to do it, I knew God was asking me to just say "yes." When I told my parents, they were ecstatic. I mean, why wouldn't they be, right? Just kidding. Humility is my greatest quality.

We put into place a two-year plan of transition, and God was in it all the way. God had spoken to my dad about this before He spoke to me about it. That makes sense, because he was the leader in the position, but it's important for you to recognize his wisdom in being farsighted. He gave me opportunities to preach, to pray and minister, and He always encouraged me. True fathers are so excited about their sons doing more, excelling, growing, and becoming all that God intends them to become. We need more of those leaders in our churches—leaders who are humble enough to recognize the season of change God is bringing about and the wisdom to look ahead and raise sons and daughters to take the lead.

The crisis of a dying church happens far too often. If we are raising spiritual sons and daughters, when sickness or tragedy occur, we should have at least two—if not four or five—people who are being mentored by the pastor, praying with the pastor, meeting with him or her regularly, being mentored to become a minister.

If you're a Christian CEO, ask God to help you think differently. You don't just have employees or staff. You have spiritual sons and daughters. If you're a pastor, ask God to help you think differently. You don't just have congregants and a leadership team or board. You have sons and daughters! You have a team of people you can affirm, guide, and provide opportunities for!

When you see them this way, you'll treat them this way. When you see your team as brothers and sisters, sons and daughters, you will treat them much better and lead them well.

You'll have more empathy when they're going through something difficult. Empathy and encouragement are at the core of our job as leaders. Instead of bossing people around, lead people forward. You lead people forward by sometimes slowing down to lean in and listen.

Why don't we see more leaders concerned with raising up leaders beneath them? Why do we have so many leaders yet so few fathers? This question is an important one. Yes, it can be hard to let go of what you've built. I'd like to give you a nugget of wisdom from Pastor Craig Groeschel: "The more you want to grow, the more you have to let go." If you were to be in a car accident tomorrow, is there anyone who comes to your mind who could take the church for you? If not, start praying about whom you could meet with weekly or even monthly to mentor. Maybe they could be your Joshua, your Timothy.

Start praying about what kind of person on staff has the potential to pastor the church—or who you'd like to have like that. Jesus often would take Peter, James, and John with Him into prayer and into circumstances the other disciples didn't enter. Who is your inner circle of three? Paul had Timothy. Moses had Joshua. Whom do you have? Who around you has potential? Who has that spark in their eye—that desire to do something for God?

Raising up other leaders is one of the most fulfilling and impactful things you can do as a Christian leader. When you do this, you move from addition to multiplication. Yes, it's hard, but it's worth it! This multiplication mindset comes from a leader who values sonship over success. After all, you want as many as possible to enter God's family!

Raising up other leaders is one of the most fulfilling and impacting things you can do as a Christian leader. When you do this, you move from addition to multiplication.

||||||||||||||||||||||||||||||||||||||||||||||||||||||||||||||||||||||||||||||||||||||||||||||||||||||||||||||||||||||||||

SONS MINISTER WITH THEIR BROTHERS

Ephesians 4 teaches us that spiritual growth—and, I would argue, leadership growth—cannot occur in isolation. If you feel you can simply "do it all" or that you "don't need" people, then you have missed the joy of doing life and ministry with brothers and sisters in Christ! You cannot be formed into the image of the Son without your brothers and sisters. Scripture makes it clear that we build one another up in our faith until we attain "unity of the faith and knowledge of the Son of God." We need each other to become the leaders God wants us to become. Many leaders miss out on this spiritual formation that God brings to them because they view other pastors or leaders as competition instead of as brothers and sisters.

Celebrate another leader's success. Grieve when they grieve. Cheer when they win! If you hear of another leader's victory and it's hard for you to celebrate, you need to think through this concept deeply and ask God to do a new work in you. Ask God to give you a new revelation of sonship and the joy of being a part of His global family.

If you hear of another leader's victory and it's hard for you to celebrate, then you need to think through this concept deeply and ask God to do a new work in you. Ask God to give you a new revelation of sonship and the joy of being a part of His global family.

||||||||||||||||||||||||||||||||||||||||||||||||||||||||||||||||||||||||||||||||||||||||||||||||||||||||||||||||||||||||||

I want to encourage you to try something that I purposefully do to illustrate this truth regarding a global family of God. I intentionally celebrate the wins of other pastors online. When I'm on Facebook and I see a pastor friend break ground on a new building or celebrate numerous people coming to salvation in service, I celebrate big with them! Why? These are my brothers and sisters expanding our family! A new house for more kids being adopted into God's family? Yes! Again, if this is a point of contention with you, if it's easy for you to find fault in other minsters instead of finding joy, then please take some time to kneel before the Lord and ask Him to do a new work in your heart.

SONS BECOME FATHERS

Christian leaders who see themselves rightly—first as sons and daughters of God—don't aim to only simply create something amazing; they also aim to father someone amazing. Rulers just die, but sons become fathers who pass on an inheritance, and their impact becomes exponential. Do you want your life to impact people for years to come? Do you want your impact to be exponential?

Leaders who only want to build some*thing* amazing sometimes arrive at their destination alone with no son to pass the baton to. As of my writing this, I've been in ministry for seventeen years, and I've seldom seen a healthy transition out of Christian leadership. It happens, but it's rare. Why? We're too busy building something and not building someone. Healthy transitions happen in Christian companies and ministries when the senior leader is not only building something but building someone. It's important to build something—a system, a program, a building, etc. It's more important to build someone. Doing so takes time: intentional time, time around a meal, time asking questions, time discussing what God is teaching you.

There are people with incredible leadership potential sitting right under your nose. Do you see them? Do you realize that you have been given a unique opportunity to be a spiritual mom or dad in their lives? Even if you can't take on that close of a relationship with them, you can give them the opportunity to grow and advance in their God-given gifts.

Can you imagine the long-term impact we'd see if more Christian leaders took on the identity of not only sonship but also fatherhood? This book was just about to be completed when I was invited to something called "The Father Initiative," now called 415 Leaders. I didn't know what I was getting into, but I simply knew God's Spirit was telling me to go to this thing to which I'd been invited. Little did I know that, often in this three-day event, God's Spirit would bring me to tears. Scott Wilson, global pastor of Oaks Church in Texas, invited us down for a weekend, in which he shared his vision to raise up spiritual fathers. He had spent quality time with a few sons and was ready to ask them to do the same. Here's how he encouraged us to father (or mother) a younger leader:

» Connect

This is not using people. You can impress from afar, but you can only impact up close. Young leaders need to know they're genuinely loved. If we can connect with our team members on a *real* level, deeper than tasks lists and projects, we can father them and show Father God's love to them!

» Affirm

This is not complimenting. This is affirming the God-like characteristics and character in them! This is prophetic. It's seeing them for who they can be and calling them up into their calling. Every team member we have working in our church or company needs the genuine affirmation of a spiritual dad or mom.

» Guide

This is not controlling. Spiritual fathers give advice, not permission. We guide our sons and daughters into godly decisions. We encourage them to pray about their decisions and at the same time guide them with biblical insight.

» Provide

This is not spoiling them. Spiritual moms and dads provide resources and tools they can work with. Our goal as leaders isn't to keep the good stuff for us. No. Spiritual moms and dads give it all away. Now, through 415 Leaders, Scott and the team are seeing many more pastors given spiritual moms and dads, which is priceless for the journey ahead!

This has been a way of living for Danielle and me—that's why this weekend was such a confirmation of what God was doing in our hearts. I strongly encourage you to pick up any of Scott Wilson's books, such as *Impact*. You'll grow in your leadership capacity and, most importantly, your heart to serve King Jesus.

Jesus didn't stop with, "Let me teach you. Let me disciple you." He compelled his disciples to partner with Him in the mission to reach people with the gospel. When He miraculously fed fifteen thousand people, He turned to His followers and said, "You feed them." He ensured they were given a chance—even a chance to fail. How much better if they could fail and learn a lesson while He was with them! Jesus carried the heart of His Father and showed that in His leadership.

Who are your spiritual sons and daughters? If you have a ministry but not a spiritual son or daughter, I encourage you to pray about who it is you could begin to mentor.

I'm so thankful for my dad and his mentoring of me over the years. There have been many times when I've gone to him for advice, and God's always spoken through him to me. His wealth of wisdom allows me to minister from a place of advantage. I can learn the lessons he's learned from thirty-six years in ministry! Why would I *not* learn those lessons from him and pay attention to how God has worked through him? Many times over, I've had a dilemma and thought back to how my dad or mom would've handled it, whether it was a difficulty with a ministry leader or simply a new challenge.

I have a few other mentors like Pastor Ed Homer, Dr. Dave Harnett, and Pastor Matt Anderson, all who have helped me when I didn't even realize I was in need of their wisdom. I am so thankful I've made time to sit with them over the years and simply be me—be open and ready to learn from them.

You and I not only have the joy and imperative of raising sons and daughters, but we need to be a spiritual son or daughter, as well. We need to return to this concept we see in scripture of family. We need someone above us and someone "below" us. We are quick to do this when we see ourselves, first, as a child of God; yet we are slow to do this when we make the mistake of thinking we have it all together and don't need help.

Gideon went through a process of becoming the leader God wanted Him to become. His process was a journey with unexpected turns and twists, and yours will be, too. What if you valued the process of becoming like Jesus and the journey of sanctification as much as you valued "the end," or the destination? I believe we need to do that. Gideon heard the voice of Father God and rose up in courage to face his enemies—those within and those without. The enemies we have within, like fear, insecurity, or pride, can sometimes be bigger than the enemies on the outside. No matter what enemy you face, God will give you the strength to face it and defeat it! With Jesus as your brother, you and I are given the sacred gift of His Holy Spirit, empowering us to do what we could not do otherwise—to be brave, lead others, lead change, endure, blow up the status quo, impact people, and build God's kingdom for God's glory! Are you willing to go through the process of a leader? Let's discuss it with a few friends.

What if you valued the process of becoming like Jesus and the journey of sanctification as much as you valued "the end," or the destination?

||||||||||||||||||||||||||||||||||||||||||||||||||||||||||||||||||||||||||||||||||||||||||||||||||||||

APPLY IT

Group Discussion Guide | P.R.O.C.E.S.S. | Week 3

» What were the excuses Gideon gave when God tapped him on the shoulder?

» Have you ever given God similar excuses? If so, what are they? That is, *I don't have enough money to do that* (the lie of scarcity when God owns it all), *I don't have enough talent to accomplish that* (the lie that God withheld good gifts from you), *I don't have the right background* (forgetting that nobody does! Only Jesus is perfect, which is why our hope is in him, not ourselves.), etc.

» What emotions might Gideon have felt when God asked him to use clay pots and trumpets instead of swords and shields? Have you ever felt silly obeying God? When?

» When Gideon did what God asked of him, God came through in miraculous ways. What might happen if we as Christian leaders begin to trust that we do hear the voice of God when we pray, seek His guidance, and begin to act in faith, no matter how abnormal the assignment may be?

» Read John 15:26–27. What does this passage tell us regarding our ability to hear God's voice?

» Read John 14:15–21. What does Jesus promise us?

» Read John 10:1–19. How is Jesus our Shepherd? Is hearing God's voice only for special leaders who are "more anointed," or does that promise also apply to you and me?

» Why do you think God reduced Gideon's already-small army to only three hundred men? A few reasons are possible: maybe to teach Gideon about his own character and develop his trust in God. Sometimes, God uses difficult situations to prove His faithfulness and His ability to save, so that He is given the glory He deserves. That's the reason God gives us in the text. God wanted to be given the credit. He deserves it!

Visit TheProcessOfALeader.com to view videos with your team so you can grow together!

Action Steps

I declare today that I can hear the voice of God for myself. I agree with the truth of scripture: that God's Spirit has been given to me and that, at times, He may ask me to do something that seems impossible.

The impossible thing that I feel God is asking me to do is: _____

_____

_____

_____

_____

CHAPTER 4

Jesus And Sonship

So you have not received a spirit that makes you fearful slaves.
Instead, you have received God's Spirit when He adopted you
as His own children! Now we call Him, "Abba, Father."
—ROMANS 8:15 (NLT)

The entire book has led up to this moment. The moment we see Jesus, the Son of God, for who He is: our brother! He is our best example of what Christian leadership looks like. He is the one who suffered in our place and enabled us to become His brothers and sisters, God's children! Before Jesus was High Priest, He was the Son of God. Before Jesus was the Savior, He was the Son of God, adored in heaven. Before Jesus was the miracle-worker on earth, He was the Son of God in heaven. From the place of sonship, Jesus was secure enough in who He was to do what He did and say what He said, even with the body and emotions of a human. His humanity was subject to the Spirit of God within Him. He is our example to follow! WOW! He was fully God and fully man, and His foremost identity was being His Father's Son. You can't read the Gospels and miss that!

His identity came solely from heaven, which is why His courage was so evident on earth. As we said earlier, God the Father was "well pleased" before Jesus ever performed a miracle or preached a sermon. At His water baptism in Matthew 3:17 (NIV), from the place of sonship, hearing, "This is my son," Jesus went out in courage to fulfill His calling with each new day's assignments.

We must learn this incredible truth as leaders. Too many leaders today lead from a place of insecurity. We all face it at times. I've spoken about it quite a bit in this book. I've seen it in my own life. I've seen it in the lives of others. Insecurity will sabotage your leadership.

Insecurity leads to poor decisions, attitudes, and outcomes. Insecurity shifts blame, pushes others down, and avoids responsibility. Leaders take responsibility and give credit.

||||||||||||||||||||||||||||||||||||||||||||||||||||||||||||||||||||||||||||||||||||||||||||||||||||||||||||||||||||||||||||||

Security in our identity as God's beloved children leads to better decisions and better outcomes. It derives from a vibrant personal relationship with Father God. Our sense of value must come from *there*—our identity in being God's child. If it doesn't, we try to find our sense of value in our assignments, gift-ings, or accomplishments. When we know our identity—who we are as God's child—we're not shaken when our assignment or season changes. When we lose a job, the plant closes, or circumstances are outside our control, we don't lose our peace or even our joy. Many people, including Christian leaders, base their sense of value on what they do instead of who they are. That has to change if we want to see more leaders last and finish strong.

Your assignments are like seasons in your life. They will come and go. Your identity as God's child won't. Your role or position in the church or company will likely change. Your identity as God's child won't. Remember, when assign-ments change, identity remains. We must not confuse identity and assignments.

God gives us the grace gifts we need to accomplish the things He wants us to accomplish in each new season. So even the gifting that allows you to do what you do is a gift from God! You cannot take any credit for it! In the words of the apostle Paul, let us only boast in the cross of Jesus Christ.

Take a look at the graph below and see how we as leaders need to start viewing ourselves.

When we know who we are—even if we're placed where we don't want to be, like Joseph—we won't lose our identity, our sense of knowing, our sense of belonging and purpose. Too often, we mix these up and feel that our sense of value is in our gifts or the title or position we have, as if it's validation of our value. Jesus determined your value at the cross, and there's nothing you can do to add to it! Realize how loved you are. Beloved, be loved!

Be found in the joy of being God's child and let your calling (mission) and assignment stem from that identity. The farther you move outward from the center of the circle, the more unique and different you are. The closer you get the center, the more you realize how alike you are. My mission and calling to inspire people to love Jesus more is similar to yours, but how it's lived out may be a bit different than yours.

My current assignment as a lead pastor is even more unique than my calling. It's likely different than your assignment. And honestly, the more I move outside this circle, the more defined my unique type of pastoral ministry is. It's as unique as my fingerprint. It's as unique as yours will be, even if you're also a lead pastor. We share our identity as children of God! The core, the center of who we both are, is family! We are sons and daughters of the living God! That never changes! Seasons will come and go, assignments will change, but I know who I am. I am a child of God. That is my identity. That is my joy. That drives everything I do.

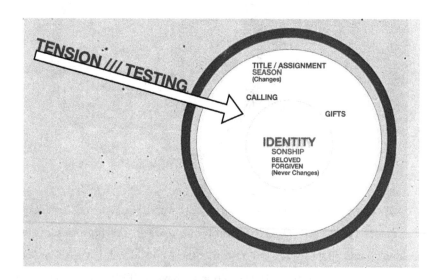

JESUS IS THE ANSWER (NOT ME)

Now that I've got my identity down and my source of joy, my mission becomes more clear.

**It's not to make more people like me; it's
to make more people like Jesus.**

My mission, if I'm a pastor, isn't to have more people in *my* church; it's to have more brothers and sisters in *His* church. If I'm a Christian businessman, I am now overjoyed when another Christian businessman has success. He is not the competition; he is a companion—he is family. His success is my success because it's *our* success—as brothers and sisters in Christ!

Jesus is the answer, not me. Jesus said in John 14:6 (NIV), "I am the way, the truth and the life. No one comes to the Father except through me." Our ultimate example of a leader who went through the process is Jesus Christ. If you're reading this book, I'm assuming you're a Christian leader or training to be. Please don't rush this section and think, *Yeah, yeah . . . I know the story of Jesus.* Don't do that. Let the Holy Spirit uncover some things in scripture that maybe you haven't seen yet. The Holy Spirit illuminates the Word of God, and in His wisdom, He will illuminate exactly what you need to face your next leadership challenges. Jesus is your brother! He's right there with you—even now, as you're reading this. Picture Him sitting beside you, smiling, encouraging you to keep going, keep leading, and keep serving!

JESUS' PROMISE

Jesus was given a promise from Father God. The Father promised Him that not only would He be able to endure the cross but that the Father would also raise Him from the dead so He could accomplish His mission in winning our salvation, bringing brothers and sisters to freedom!

Jesus saw Abraham offer his son Isaac after a three-day journey. Jesus watched from heaven with His Father as this prophetic picture unfolded. He knew that, although He would suffer horribly, Father God would deliver Him from death. Jesus was given a promise. This promise included being returned to His rightful place, back at the right hand of the Father. Like Joseph, He was given all authority and seated at the right hand! Like Joseph prepared a place for his brothers to live, so has Jesus prepared a place for us! Joseph forgave His brothers and invited them into His blessing, and Jesus does this same thing for us!

John 1 describes Jesus as being the life and the light of all mankind. He was before all things and in Him all things were created! Colossians 1:15 describes Him as the visible image of the invisible God, the firstborn of all creation. He's the firstborn of all creation because He's bringing more children into God's family! Hebrews 1:3-4 (ESV) describes Jesus as the heir of all things, Creator of all things, and the radiance of God's glory! He was given a promise that He would purify people and then be given back His throne: "After making purification for sins, He sat down at the right hand of the Majesty on high, having become as much superior to angels as the name He has inherited is more excellent than theirs."

Jesus agreed to come, knowing that He would suffer in our place and take our blame. Jesus was promised by the Father that He would be given many brothers and sisters. We see that in John 17 very clearly. The victory that Jesus won for us enables us to live and walk in love. As leaders, this is incredibly important! How often does fear inhibit our leadership when love is trying to propel us forward?

When you walk in the mindset of fear, like Romans 8 speaks about, you're not living in the truth of what Jesus won. Jesus came and died on that cross and rose from that grave so that you would no longer live as a fearful slave but as a child of God, Jesus' brother or sister! This was the promise given to Him by the Father. God made good on that promise!

**That revelation of our identity as God's child
should give us the courage to face anything!**

||||||||||||||||||||||||||||||||||||||||||||||||||||||||||||||||||||||||||||||||||||||||||||||||||||||||||||||||||

JESUS FACED REALITY

When the problems and heartaches of God's people were in the face of Jesus, He didn't hide. He didn't shrink back. You may say, "Well, He was Jesus, the Son of God." Yes, but He was also fully man. While this is hard for us to understand, the Bible states it as truth—that Jesus was fully man and fully God, therefore He was "tempted in every way like we are tempted"—that includes being tempted to not live up to that calling on His life. We know He was tempted in the Garden of Gethsemane to give up. We know He was tempted in the desert to give in. We can also infer that He may have even been tempted to never begin. Think about it: when we saw John the Baptist, what were Jesus' thoughts in that moment?

> » Here we go!
> » This is it!
> » It's getting real now!
> » Everything is about to change if I state who I am. I'll go from carpenter to heretic in their eyes. I'll go from just another Jewish man to a target really fast. I know the Pharisees will hate me. I'm sure God's people may not even accept me.
> » If I allow Him to baptize me, it will begin. This is the turning point. This is it!

Sometimes, we forget the humanity Jesus walked in. He was teaching us in every moment. If He can do it, we can look to Him, and we can do it, too! If He can suppress physical hunger in order to fast, we can do it, too. If He can ignore the criticism of the mob and stay on mission, then we can, too!

Jesus faced the real problems of his day. He didn't cower at the religious leaders and their manipulation or intimidation. He didn't cave to politics or peer pressure. He didn't stop preaching or healing when they told Him to. He invited people into His Father's family while at the same time confronting the sins He saw. Jesus faced reality.

When Jesus stood in heaven and was asked by the Father to go to earth to save us, we can only imagine that moment. We can only imagine Jesus agreeing to that journey, that process, that pain. Why did He agree? He knew the Father would make good on the promise!

When Jesus faced Pharisees, who were just plain ugly on the inside, He confronted their arrogance and told them, "You are whitewashed tombs, clean on the outside and yet full of only death on the inside." He knew what any leader knows: you can't fix a problem until you identify and acknowledge the problem. When Jesus saw people stealing in the temple courts, He knocked over their tables and made it clear that the temple was to be a place of worship and prayer.

The key to facing your reality is to be observant and honest. If you avoid the problems in front of you and you are the leader, your potential impact stops dead right there.

||||||||||||||||||||||||||||||||||||||||||||||||||||||||||||||||||||||||||||||||||||||||||||||||||||||||||||||||||

Your leadership stops in its tracks. Your team looks to you to address the issue, not ignore it. The leader's first role is to define reality; his second role is to offer a picture of a better one.

When Jesus faced obstacles like the religious leaders who set out to trap Him in His own words and even to kill Him, He would remain unwavering in His mission. When you make a decision for your team, it's possible that some won't agree. They'll have a decision to make. After you hear them out and discuss their ideas or concerns, they'll still need to come into alignment with your decision so the team can move forward in unity. If they don't understand, do your best to help them grasp your motives and the full scope of the decision. If they still refuse to align, you have a new reality to face. Don't ignore it. Bring gentle but firm correction and give an opportunity to move forward together.

If you ignore it, division will begin, and that person will cause mistrust and misalignment in others.

Jesus didn't perceive these obstacles from the Pharisees or even the occasional backlash from his own disciples as barriers that would stop Him from going to the cross or from healing the sick and preaching the truth. He was faithful to continue all the way to the cross. For those who refused to see His heart and accept His mission, He told them the truth in love and kept going.

Jesus endured to the end. Hebrews tells us that Jesus is the firstborn of many and that He is our example of what it means to lay down our lives and pick up our cross, knowing that God will bring resurrection. Jesus had endurance! He faced the painful reality that the disciples whom He'd befriended and mentored would betray Him. He didn't live in denial, and He certainly didn't write them off. He endured in His mission.

When Peter denied even knowing Jesus, He was so loving and forgiving that He came and met Peter on the lakeside and made Him breakfast! Jesus essentially said, "We're still friends." And then, to top it off, Jesus said to Peter, "Feed my sheep," as if to communicate, "I still want you in the ministry although you blew it. Look, I know what you did, but I'm not here to talk about that. I'm here to ask you this one simple question: 'Do you love Me? If so, then feed my sheep.'" Jesus was saying to Peter, "Give everyone who is searching for truth the truth. Give them the Bread of Life. Give them the hope they need. Give them JESUS! Don't give up on the mission. You're still in this! You're still on my team!"

Peter was inevitably shocked that Jesus would still include him in His inner circle. He must've assumed that he had blown it completely—that Jesus no longer had need of him. Maybe this is why he was alone. We can't know that for sure. But what we can know for sure is that Jesus gave Peter another chance. Why? He loved Peter. He loved the people who needed to hear from Peter. The mission was too big to allow unforgiveness to hinder progress.

I found a helpful article titled "7 Practical Thoughts on Forgiveness in Leadership," written by Steve Tillis,[3] on the leader's need to forgive and move forward. I think it'll help you as much as it helped me.

1) Forgiveness requires so much energy that you can help yourself by having a soft heart and thick skin. If you constantly take everything personally you won't have any energy left to forgive in the situations that really hurt. Learn to let some stuff roll off your back. Focus on the people and issues that really need forgiveness.

2) Forgiveness is easier when you don't define the person by what they have done to you. The person that is hurting you is most likely a decent Christian who is caught up in the middle of a volatile situation. Don't judge their whole life on what they are doing now to you. Take the kind of perspective on their life that you would want them to take on yours.

3) Forgiveness is a standard by which you can measure your Christian spiritual growth. How often do you say "I'm sorry?" It shows humility toward God and love for others when we are quick to apologize. When we wait to say "I'm sorry" or we don't grant forgiveness quickly, we are living from a source of pride.

4) Forgiveness has a powerful way of taking the steam out of an argument. How many conflicts become inflated because people won't apologize? I've found that those people who are coming to the office for a big battle are disarmed by a prompt and sincere apology.

5) Forgiveness very rarely needs to be accompanied with an unsolicited explanation. This is tough because we always want to make an excuse or give a rationale for our behavior. Just practice the discipline of asking for forgiveness and stopping. To be sure, sometimes the explanation is required but most often it's not. Practicing this will help you

---

3   Steve Tillis, "7 Practical Thoughts on Forgiveness in Leadership," Rookie Preacher, 7 Dec. 2019, https://www.rookiepreacher.com/7-practical-thoughts-on-forgiveness-in-leadership/.

even when you are the one who has been hurt. Because in ministry sometimes you can't give the other party all the information you know.

6) Forgiveness is the natural overflow of a life saturated in the gospel. This is more than a catchy statement, it's true. Walk your thoughts through the components of the gospel concerning the situation. Remember that God's original intention was for us to live in constant dependence on him. Remember that the problem you are having could be birthed in a lie someone believed. Remember that Christ came to redeem the worst of us. Remember that we can be restored. We see in the Garden that we were made for fellowship.

7) Forgiveness does not mean forgetting, it means releasing. It's not profitable to try and force yourself to not remember being hurt. What you can do is choose not to hold the offense against the person. This is not easy, but it is the most Christ-like thing you can do in life and ministry. The Holy Spirit does have the power to help you supernaturally forget the offense. But don't think that just because you remember that you haven't forgiven. If you can truly desire that your offender is blessed by the Lord, then you're walking in the freedom of forgiveness.

SONSHIP

Jesus grew up knowing the promise within Him, the destiny He had in revealing the Father to all mankind, but He held it in all those years! Let's take another look at how He began His ministry:

> *Now when all the people were baptized, and when Jesus also had been baptized and was praying, the heavens were opened, and the Holy Spirit descended on Him in bodily form, like a dove; and a voice came from heaven, "You are my beloved Son; with you I am well pleased."*
>
> —LUKE 3:21–22

Before Jesus entered ministry, He humbled Himself and was baptized by His cousin, John. In that moment, God spoke to Jesus in an audible voice! He said, "You are my beloved Son. With you I am well pleased."

God the Father was well pleased with Jesus before He ever performed any miracles or preached any sermons. The same is true of you. Because of what Jesus has done in making you His brother or sister and allowing His nature to be seen in you, you too, are loved. You give God pleasure *before* you perform. Simply being God's gives God pleasure. Before you preach a great sermon, perform perfectly as a CEO, COO, or executive pastor, before you do anything *for* God, God already looks upon you with incredible love. He's proud of you because when He sees you, He sees Jesus!

Do you realize the power of this statement toward Jesus? God the Father showed His approval and pleasure before Jesus did any "ministering" or miracles or leading. What does this tell you? Jesus could operate without any insecurity in His ministry because, before He was a minster, He was a son—a *beloved* son!

HOW ABOUT YOU?

Have you let God affirm your identity as His child lately? Have you heard Him say, "This is my child in whom I am well pleased"? Have you let His love push out all insecurity and need for approval or affirmation from people? What about Jesus' tender heart? Have you let the Father put that tender heart of grace in you?

What can you learn from Jesus about His willingness to forgive His team and still partner with them in the work the Father had given Him? What do you think about Jesus' tenacious endurance? How did endurance play a role in the life of Jesus as a leader? How are these two concepts connected: endurance and forgiveness? Stop and think about it. If you're going through this book in a team, spark up a short conversation asking one another, "If Jesus forgave His own teammates in order to accomplish the mission and endure, what does that mean for us as colleagues when we have conflict?"

We said early on that "success is personal obedience to God's directives. It's obedience to God's voice." Success isn't about being seen as important. Success isn't about being the smartest person in the room; it's about being faithful to your assignments to fulfill your promise from the Father.

No matter how it plays out. No matter who agrees or disagrees. No matter if everyone responds to your plea to action or if only 10 percent respond. Success is obedience. Jesus was successful because He was obedient to His Father's request to leave heaven, be born a human, endure rejection, teach about God's love and, ultimately, give His life on a cross. The Father asked Him. Jesus obeyed. Jesus succeeded and endured because He knew His identity as His Father's Son.

It's possible that you need to reframe your life's goal. Is it to be a successful leader in the eyes of people? Is it to make *your* church or company successful? Is it to be known around the world or among your peers? Is it growth simply for the sake of growth? Or is your goal to make the Father revealed? Is it to make Jesus known? Those who come into that revelation find the greatest joy, for they find what life is all about. Those leaders find that Jesus is their brother and their ultimate goal in life is to make the Father known. They discover the best way to do that is to follow Jesus' example in serving others and in being in right relationship to the Father.

Leaders in the kingdom of God know that their first priority is to be a brother of Jesus, a child of God. When the leader remembers this, he or she remains humble and eager to learn. Leaders who are humble and eager to learn are actually more readily followed.

Dr. Townsend of the Leadership Institute did a national poll of employees and team members. They found that the majority of people said, "They would rather follow a leader who admits their mistakes and shows their eagerness to improve over a leader who is never vulnerable."

Jesus allowed His disciples to see that He was weak in the Garden. Why would He do that? Think about it. As leaders, we often put our "best foot forward," or at the very least attempt to hide our errors or shortcomings. What if we flipped the script? What if we followed the example of Jesus, our brother, and let them see when we are weak and in need of the Father's help?

I'm not suggesting we display every insecure thought or missed task to our employees or team. Some discretion is advised. But I am suggesting an appropriate level of honesty and vulnerability. If you miss the quarterly goal that you set, own it. Real leaders take responsibility; they don't constantly blame others. If you were assigned four things in the meeting and you only completed three, be willing to say, "Guys, I'm sorry, I only got three of the four things assigned to me done. Please forgive me. I'll do my best to get better at managing my daily tasks."

That humility will go a long way in showing your team that, "Yes, their leader is also human. Show them that you're eager to improve and willing to grow. That humility is contagious and will spark a desire in everyone to also be willing to be honest and dependent upon the Father for strength.

Paul said, "In my weakness, His strength is made perfect." When he said that, do you think the apostles and spiritual sons like Timothy or Barnabas thought to themselves, *Well, I'm not following Paul anymore! Clearly, he's a weakling!*? No. Instead, they likely thought, *Wow! It's so refreshing to follow someone who knows they're not perfect; that only Christ is perfect. He needs God's strength for today, just like me.*

If anything, your humility in moments of failure or weakness draws your team closer to you and emboldens their desire to serve alongside you. After all, now they're alongside you and not so much behind you.

There are many reasons why I've admired Abraham Lincoln. He simply stands out to me as the greatest president our nation ever had. Maybe it's because he helped abolish slavery. Maybe it's because he tried his hand at entrepreneurship and had the courage to try just about anything. Maybe it's because of his faith in the Lord. Do you know where the nickname "Honest Abe" came from? It was the slogan used to mark his 1860 political campaign, but it was derived from his reputation as a small-town businessman. You see, he started a General Store with a friend and that friend became a drunkard, forfeiting all his responsibilities to Abe. Abe lost the store and yet paid back every penny of the debt incurred, a total of $1,100. Keep in mind, this was 1860, so that's a huge chunk of change!

> *Without doubt, honesty has always been the best policy.*
> —TOM PETERS

> *Managers do things right. Leaders do the right thing.*
> —BENNIS AND NANUS

Jesus exemplified integrity and character at all times. It was His authenticity and integrity that inspired those fishermen, tax collectors, and doctors to keep following Him. I'm sure the miracles may have hooked them (pun intended), but it was Jesus' authentic character that kept them. In the same way, you can impress people for a while with your gifts or abilities, but it's your character and trustworthiness that will cause them to stay for the long run.

I heard about a church recently where the staff culture was somewhat of a revolving door. That can be expected at McDonalds or Subway. But that shouldn't be expected where you lead. If they can't trust you, they won't follow you for long. If they don't feel that you genuinely care about their well-being, their future, and their desires, then they won't follow you for long. We've all heard it said, "It's lonely at the top." That may be true for most leaders, but that does not have to be true for you. I believe we should aim to reach goals together and celebrate those mountaintop moments together. In Acts, they were following Jesus together as each person used their grace gift to lead and love others.

Keep in mind that there are times when team members do leave, and that's expected. Not everyone will stay with you through your entire leadership journey. It's proven that, with new leadership—whether it's in a church or company—not everyone will stay. Some may give it a go for a few years but not be able to connect with the new pastor or senior leader the way they did with the previous one. And that's okay.

The second reason some people may leave your team is that a new vision is given. When a new vision is laid out, it's possible some team members can't see themselves in that preferred picture of the future. And that's okay. It doesn't make them bad people, and it doesn't make you a bad leader. Not everyone will make the whole journey with you. That's just a reality of life. We all have different seasons and assignments, as we mentioned earlier, and some people on your team may be prompted by the Lord to enter a new season. That's okay because, as we established earlier, God's family is BIG! When they tell you, don't try to control them or convince them to stay. Simply bless them, encourage them, and let them know how thankful you are that they were with you for that season of the journey.

I want to make this concept of sonship a bit more tangible. Here are eleven signs of sonship. There will likely be one or two that bring a loving conviction to your heart. Ask the Holy Spirit to help you in this area and commit to change.

ELEVEN SIGNS OF SONSHIP

1) A PRAYER LIFE

A Christian leader who grasps sonship has a strong prayer life; they have dedicated time with their faith regularly. For Jesus, it was His alone time in the mornings with the Father. He often would find a quiet place to pray. The Father would give Him energy and encouragement. The Spirit would give Him strength to face the week ahead.

For Jesus, He had disciples whom He viewed at teammates. "I no longer call you servants but friends...." He said to them in John 15:15. When teaching them to pray, He said, "Our Father...." He truly viewed Himself as their brother!

Jesus certainly had "takers," people who would only show up hoping for another free meal. He had people who were truly in need of forgiveness, too— people truly wanting to repent and accept the kingdom of God. That was His mission, and that had to be beautiful to see! But even Jesus didn't spend His time only with those who would simply take from Him or drain Him. He valued His friendships with Peter, James, John, and the crew. He valued His time alone with the Father. You and I would be wise to follow suit.

2) COURAGE TO LEAD

The courage to lead comes from knowing that you are called by God and that this whole thing wasn't your idea in the first place!

For consider your calling, brothers: not many of you were wise according to worldly standards, not many were powerful, not many were of noble birth. But God chose what is foolish in the world to shame the wise; God chose what is weak in the world to shame the strong; God chose what is low and despised in the world, even things that are not, to bring to nothing things that are, so that no human being might boast in the presence of God. And because of him you are in Christ Jesus, who became to us wisdom from God, righteousness and sanctification and redemption, so that, as it is written, "Let the one who boasts, boast in the Lord."

—1 CORINTHIANS 1:26-31 (ESV)

And I, when I came to you, brothers, did not come proclaiming to you the testimony of God with lofty speech or wisdom. For I decided to know nothing among you except Jesus Christ and him crucified. And I was with you in weakness and in fear and much trembling, and my speech and my message were not in plausible words of wisdom,

but in demonstration of the Spirit and of power, so that your faith
might not rest in the wisdom of men but in the power of God.
—CORINTHIANS 1:2-5

God chose you and me despite our problems, failures, fears, and inadequacies! In our weakness, His strength is made perfect! Don't think for a minute that you chose the wrong thing in choosing Christian leadership, for you didn't choose it—God chose you! Scripture is clear that it is God who put leaders in positions of leadership.

"God changes times and seasons. He removes kings and sets up kings."
—DANIEL 2:21

"There is no authority except from God and those
that exist have been instituted by God."
—ROMANS 13:1 (ESV)

Leader, it's likely that you've already started. If you haven't, I'm asking you to be brave enough to start. It will always be there until you respond and say "yes!" to it. The calling is "without repentance," scripture says.

Say, "Yes!" to the call of God on your life.
That calling will never leave your heart, no
matter how hard you try to run from it.

Once you start Christian leadership, I'm asking you to keep your eyes on Jesus, the Author and Finisher of your faith. He is the One who called you into this thing! He is faithful to complete the work He started in you! He promised it in His Word! Keep your head up. You can and you will finish strong! Remember that you are a CHILD OF GOD! I'm not asking you to lead in your own strength but in the strength and power of Jesus Christ! Paul says that this power works within you to complete the mission in front of you!

When we read John 14-17 and Matthew 28:16-20, we learn that Jesus commissions us to go in His authority and to make disciples. He tells us that we can hear His voice! He is our Good Shepherd and wants to speak and empower us to build His kingdom wherever we are—in the pulpit or in the corner office—in the church or in the marketplace. Too many leaders don't realize that they've been given all authority to make disciples and change their cities for Jesus! They stay in their comfort zone. They don't pray for the sick to be healed. They don't expect the sick to be healed because they don't truly believe Jesus rose from the dead. If they did, they would know that Jesus has all power to heal. Maybe you do believe Jesus is who He says He is, but you need to be reminded today! Jesus has given you all authority to love everyone who crosses your path. Jesus has given you all authority to display His kindness to a hurting world, caring for orphaned children, widows, and the poor. Jesus has given you all authority to stand by your convictions that derive from the Word of God. Be bold. Be brave.

3) COURAGE TO CONFRONT

Leaders who are first a child of God have the courage to confront. Leaders who are more concerned with success than sonship will shy away from any sort of conflict that needs resolved. True leaders, leaders in God's kingdom, will know that they are first and foremost a son/daughter of God, and in that security, they will be able to make the tough calls that need to be made. From a place of security, we make our toughest decisions. From a place of knowing that we are loved by Father God, we can confront people and make needed changes. From a place of knowing that we are loved by Father God, we can avoid the fear of man that paralyzes us.

One of the lines my mentor in Bible college, Richard Crisco, shared often was, "Leaders care enough to confront." Leaders who follow Jesus' example will have the courage to give the truth in love. This means that sometimes, after giving that truth, people will leave. That's okay. Of course, we don't want them to leave. We never want our followers or leadership team members to leave. But when confronted with the truth of God's Word, people are given a chance to either surrender to it or to demand their own way. You can't control how they respond, but you can control your response, your heart, and your actions as the leader. You can hold a high bar of integrity and yet open arms of forgiveness like Jesus did. What you can't afford to do, however, is ignore when someone is blatantly sinning. In that moment, it is your job to privately speak to them, give them the truth in love, and give them a chance to explain and repent and hopefully be restored if they're repentant.

*You can download a free eBook called *Truth & Love in Confrontation* from my website, www.JordanBiel.com. It's an excerpt from my first book, *Truth & Love*.

4) HUMILITY

Leaders, you must know that you can't lead others if you can't lead yourself. The first person you lead is the one in the mirror. Let the Holy Spirit do His work of sanctification, bringing you to a place where you think, act, and lead more like Jesus—like a humble servant. Sonship is what it's all about! Remember what Romans 10:12-16 (ESV) says about humility:

Love one another with brotherly affection. Outdo one another in showing honor. Do not be slothful in zeal, be fervent in spirit, serve the Lord. Rejoice in hope, be patient in tribulation, be constant in prayer. Contribute to the needs of the saints and seek to show hospitality. Bless those who persecute you; bless and do not curse them. Rejoice with those who rejoice, weep with those who weep. Live in harmony with one another. Do not be haughty, but associate with the lowly. Never be wise in your own sight.

There is nothing more repelling than pride. There are various forms of pride. Spiritual pride. Intellectual pride. Pride says, "I'm smarter, more spiritual, better . . . than you." Pride reveals itself in rolling eyes, smirks, and dishonoring comments about other team members or the leader. God is pretty clear how He feels about pride.

"Everyone who is arrogant in heart is an abomination to the Lord; be assured, he will not go unpunished. By steadfast love and faithfulness iniquity is atoned for, and by the fear of the Lord one turns away from evil."
—PROVERBS 16:5–6 (ESV)

"Pride goes before destruction, and a haughty spirit before a fall."
—PROVERBS 16:18 (ESV)

"There are six things that the Lord hates, seven that are an abomination to him: haughty eyes, a lying tongue, and hands that shed innocent blood, a heart that devises wicked plans, feet that make haste to run to evil, a false witness who breathes out lies, and one who sows discord among brothers."
—PROVERBS 6:16–19 (ESV)

It's interesting to me that, when the Lord lists the things He hates, He doesn't include rape or theft. Of course, those are terrible things, and I'm in no way belittling them. I'm just making the point. What does the Lord list for His hate list? Haughty eyes, lying, murder, a malicious heart, sin, lying (again), and one who causes division among brothers. God is quite clear that He disdains pride that causes wickedness, division, rolling eyes, and haughty looks. These should never be characteristics of Christian leaders. We should walk with a sense of humility that truly sees others as more valuable than ourselves. This leads me to the next sign of sonship.

5) GRACIOUSNESS

Leaders who have the Spirit of Jesus in them are filled with grace; they're willing to forgive and to give grace and honor to the leaders who serve beneath them on their teams. We all will have moments when one of our staff drops the ball. A true leader never embarrasses anyone by correcting them in public, especially a teammate or another leader. Anyone who does that is struggling with some insecurity and feels the need to appear powerful. The exception, of course, is when the leader needs to hold someone on the team accountable in a team/staff meeting where adjustments simply need to be made on minor tasks. Course correction in a safe environment on a team is one thing. Embarrassing someone in front of a group of people is another, and it's totally uncalled for.

I've been in the room when someone feels the need to embarrass another team member, and that doesn't come from the Holy Spirit's leading. Also, I'm a part of two groups on Facebook where thousands of Christian leaders are learning from one another, networking ideas, and so forth. All too often, I've seen a post where a pastor or worship leader throws a teammate under the bus. This is simply not how Jesus would want you and me to lead. If we're upset with someone on our team, we're given clear instructions in Mathew 5 and 18, like we talked about earlier, on how and when to confront someone with whom we have an issue. In front of a group of people is never the appropriate environment.

What would cause a leader to lack grace and to lash out at people from the stage? The *lack* of sonship. You see, if I as the leader value sonship over success, if I know that I am fully loved as a child of Father God and that nothing could take away the love of God that is in Christ Jesus, then I don't feel the need to appear right, powerful, or smarter in front of a crowd. I don't feel the need to belittle someone else to make myself look more spiritual. Those immature thought patterns have a way of simply leaving our mind as we are transformed by the love of Christ, our brother and Lord. When the Spirit of God bears witness with our spirit that we are adopted and have become children of God, heirs of the kingdom, we are so filled with joy that we no longer need affirmation from "the crowd." This leads me to our next sign of sonship.

6) SECURITY

We've talked about this often in this book. As King David said in Psalm 23 (ESV), "The Lord is my Shepherd; I shall not want...." If you *want* recognition to the point of needing it to feel important or loved, then you need a deeper revelation of sonship—a deeper revelation of what Father God has done for you in calling you His child!

We all want recognition to a degree—especially creative recognition—and most leaders are somewhat the creative type. We get a sense of identity by what we create. And that's, in some ways, normal. We find joy in the making, in the work. I think because God is creative, we are to be creative. Because God found joy in creating, we find joy in creating. Because God found joy in looking at what He made and saying, "It is good," I think we can find joy in looking at the team, product, or service we offer and saying, "It is good." But the problem lies in *needing* that affirmation from others. You must let God your Father be the sole source of information on who you are. If you know whose you are, you'll know who you are. And if you know who you are, you won't need others to tell you who you are. You won't need affirmation from people to be happy.

All of us can usually spot an insecure leader when we see one. They fish for compliments, namedrop, accuse others, and blame any problem on anyone other them themselves as much as possible. They never take responsibility.

Be secure not in *your* achievements, but in Christ's. Because Jesus became poor, you can become rich toward God. Because Jesus was rejected, you can be accepted. Because Jesus was filled with sorrow and betrayed by those closest to Him, you can be filled with joy and even given friends so great that only God Himself could provide them. Because Jesus went to the cross and rose to new life, you can be given new life! Celebrate and live in the joy of what He has already done! Don't strive to find joy in only what you will do. Don't be the older brother seen in Luke 15. Be gracious, knowing that you too have been given grace.

7) GRATEFULNESS

We should be the most grateful people, for God has adopted us into His family! God has taken a risk on us, empowered us, and anointed us to serve alongside Him to bring people into their destiny. Yes, it's okay to find joy in reaching your goals and creating something truly special. That creative spirit and that drive to lead were put there by God. *But don't let your ambition cloud your adoption. Before you're a leader, you're a son.* And not just any son, but a son of the Most High God! WOW! What a joy and what a privilege!

If you'll let this truth settle in deep within you, everything will change. You'll live a happier life, because your joy won't be contingent upon others' actions but will be found within. If you grasp this sonship thing, you'll be inspiring people to join your cause and to share your idea without you even knowing it, drawing people toward your vision instead of begging them to join it. A man or woman who understands adoption to God and then finds a unique vision from their Father God will have no shortage of followers. A man or a woman who wants to lead but has yet to find joy in being a child of God will only lead for a while—then the passion will fade when the numbers are low, when the reports are in, and when it doesn't look good. That's when many leaders quit. That's when many leaders don't endure.

A leader who is first a son or daughter of God can endure accusations and sleep well at night. A leader who is first a son or daughter of God can face obstacles and keep their head up. A leader who understands sonship can face the reality of their company or their church, admit the problems that need addressed, and begin to tackle them one by one, with or without 100 percent approval of everyone around them. Why? They know they're 100 percent approved by God.

Your calling to ministry from your Father will sustain you through every trial and obstacle. Knowing you're first a child of God will keep you grounded when you're praised and keep you encouraged when you're blamed.

You must know that, above all else and before all else, you are loved by Father God. Whether you "fail" or "succeed" in your eyes or the eyes of others, you are loved by your Heavenly Father, and nothing you can ever do will change that! So why not go for it? Why not take that big risk you're thinking about? I know there's something burning in your soul to accomplish! I know there's a passion to reach a destiny within you! I know it! Otherwise, you wouldn't be reading this book! You have a destiny to reach, a Promised Land to take possession of, a place God has already said, "I have given you," and now you must simply believe it! After all, if you're loved as a child of God and this thing you try to lead doesn't work out, it's okay! It's not the end of the world. Why? You're a son! A daughter. A child of the Most High God! That, my friend, is something to smile about!

While the men and women we read about in scripture inspire us, we shouldn't aim to simply be like them. We shouldn't think, *I could just be as courageous as David* . . . or, *If I could just be as determined as Nehemiah*. . . . We must remember that all of these leaders served as a type of Christ—a foreshadowing of the majesty of Jesus—Jesus, who came as the suffering servant to save us and be the real hero.

I love what Edmund Clowney wrote in his book, *Preaching Christ in All of Scripture*:

> *I first believe in the one to whom David points; I'll never become like David at all. It is not the stories of individuals who point us to Christ. The*

redemptive purpose of God is to redeem a people and renew a creation. There, all the major events in the history of the formation of the people of God also point us to Christ.

Jesus is the one through whom all people are created (John 1). Thus the creation story itself points forward to the new creation in Christ. Jesus is the one who went through temptation and probation in the wilderness. Thus the story of the fall points forward to the successful probation and active obedience of Christ. The exodus story points forward to the true exodus Jesus led for His people through His death (Luke 9:31). He led them not just out of economic and political bondage but out of bondage to sin and death itself through His death and resurrection! The wandering in the wilderness and the exile to Babylon point forward to Jesus' homelessness and the wandering and wilderness temptation, culminating in his suffering as the scapegoat outside the gate. He underwent the ultimate exile that fulfilled the righteousness of God fully.

Jesus is very literally the true Israel, the seed (Galatians 3:16-17). He is the only one who is faithful to the covenant. He is the remnant of one. He fulfills all the obligations of the covenant for all who believe. When Hosea talks about the exodus of Israel from Egypt, he says "Out of Egypt, I called my son" (Hosea 11:1, ESV). Hosea calls all of Israel 'my son.'"

Why? Jesus is the SON who makes YOU a son or a daughter of God! Jesus is the new human who set all things right! Jesus taught us what it means to be obedient to the Father and fully submissive to His will. Jesus is the culmination of all things beautiful, the Rose of Sharon, the Bright Morning Star, the one who captures the heart of His beloved (Song of Solomon). Jesus did what you and I cannot do to earn what you and I can never earn. Jesus won for us freedom from the bondage of sin and gave us right standing with *Abba*, Father. Now our hearts rightfully cry out to God *"Abba*, Father."

Sonship is what life is all about. Sonship must become more important to you than success. Sonship is the most incredible revelation any human can experience. We don't know who we really are—yes, even we "strong" leaders—until we receive the Father's loving smile: the smile that says, "You're my child, and I love you no matter what!"

Swiss theologian Hans Urs von Balthasar captures this in an image that is supernatural yet also natural. He says:

After a mother has smiled at her child for many days and weeks, she finally receives her child's smile in response. She has awakened love in the heart of her child and as the child awakens to love, it also awakens to knowledge. Knowledge comes into play because the play of love had already begun beforehand, initiated by the mother, the transcendent.[4]

While this is a natural picture—something we see all the time around us when a mom births her child—it's a supernatural picture of God's love that awakens us. That's what Hans is arguing here. He continues:

God interprets Himself to man as love in the same way: He radiates love, which kindles the light of love in the heart of man, and it's precisely this light that allows man to perceive this —the absolute LOVE. 'For it is the God who said 'Let light shine out of the darkness' who has shone in our heart to give the light of the knowledge of the glory of God in the face of Christ." (2 Corinthians 4:6) In this face (the face of Jesus) the primal foundation of being smiles at us as a mother and as a father. Insofar as we are His creatures, the seed of love lies dormant within us as the image of God. Just as no child can be awakened to love without being loved, so too no human heart can come to an understanding of God without the free gift of His grace—in the image of His Son.

---

4   Hans Urs von Balthasar, *Love Alone is Credible*

Wow! The bright, beautiful smile of an overjoyed mother awakens love in the heart of the child. This picture, this metaphor that Hans gives us of how we relate to God, is powerful because it's so tangible. All of us have seen it. Especially in the world of social media, we find more and more parents posting pictures of that first moment when mom holds her newborn baby. There's nothing like it! That face, that emotion that's captured, is beyond words. It's beyond anything an artist could ever create.

Hans was right. We only are awakened to life and love when we look into the face of God, our Creator—more specifically, into the face of Jesus. For Jesus is the perfect image of the invisible God!

You may be tempted to believe that you will one day be happy when you achieve success in your leadership. When your company is "big." When your church is "big." Then, *then*, you will be filled with joy. No, my friend.

We come to life, and our hearts are awakened by love when we behold the face of Jesus, the Son of God! That's true of those you lead and that's true for you and me. The Son of God came to make more sons and daughters—to awaken the children of God to the love of their Father. This is the most beautiful, stunning, life-changing revelation in my opinion.

8) CHRIST-CENTERED SPEECH

Jesus and His work must be at the center of every Christian leader's messaging. Jesus came to restore hope, give life, redeem His creation, and buy back the sons of man! He came to set wrong right, to forgive every one of us of every sin—every single sin that separated us from our Holy God. He taught us to forgive one another and extend his government, His law of love, to everyone around us. For us as leaders, that means even those who criticize our leadership or mock our decisions. Love will find a way to honor even your critics. Love is at the core of sonship.

Before you are an amazing leader, before you bring salvation to others, before you bring them aid, rescue, wisdom, or help of any sort, you must realize that you find 100 percent of your identity in being a son or daughter of God. When we look at the Bible, cover to cover, we find that sonship is the goal.

Does God want to partner with you to rescue people, use you, work through you as if you were a conduit of his power, and see you as an ambassador, a royal deliverer of the King's message? Yes! But more importantly than all of that is to Him that you find your true identity as being a child of God, a son of our Heavenly Father! More important than you becoming an amazing leader is that you find joy in being a child of God. When the applause goes silent, when the ratings or views are low, when criticism is coming your way, your identity will not be shaken and your joy will not be missing if you'll come to understand this truth. Your greatest joy is found in your true identity: a child of a loving Father. You are fully known and fully loved. You are a brother or a sister of Jesus Himself, who is the firstborn among many!

What we find in all of these heroes, be they prophets, priests or kings, is a foreshadowing of Jesus, the Son of God. Jesus is the hero of every story. Jesus, the Son of God, is the main character in the story. Jesus landed the lead role, and you and I are the supporting cast. If you fail to understand this and you're inwardly striving to be the center of attention, you will live your life in constant frustration, unable to pinpoint why you can't find joy. You'll wonder why, at the center of your being, you can't find peace when you lay your head down at night—even if you accomplish great things for God.

This is a subtle thing, but it's about an underlying message that does come through to those you lead. Not everyone will pick up on it, but the discerning will. If you're a minister, you are communicating many things when you preach. These things are said overtly, but many of them are communicated subconsciously. You're communicating one of the following:

Our church is amazing!

My sermon is amazing!

I am amazing!

or

Jesus is amazing!

Your message comes through in your tone, demeanor, and what you literally say. If your heart is sincere and you're truly so grateful that Jesus saved you from your sin, then your humility and passion will come through. They'll feel what they felt with John the Baptist. He was certain who he was and who he wasn't. His message was clear: *Repent and be saved! Jesus is the Savior, not me.*

Why is it that some Christian leaders and ministers lose their joy? It's because they've begun to value success over sonship. One thing can give you peace at night and joy in your soul, whether you're leading ten thousand or ten, and that is knowing God is your Father and Jesus is your brother! John Calvin, like all theologians including you and me, didn't get it all right, but he certainly did when he said this:

Christ is Isaac, the beloved son of the father who was offered as a sacrifice but nevertheless did not succumb to the power of death. He is Jacob, the watchful shepherd who has such great care for the sheep which He guards. He is the good and compassionate brother Joseph who in his glory was not ashamed to acknowledge his brothers however lowly and abject their condition. He is the great sacrifice for us! He is the King and Priest Melchizedek who has offered an eternal sacrifice once for all. He is the sovereign lawgiver Moses writing His law on the tablets of our hearts by His Spirit. He is the faithful captain and guide Joshua to lead us to the Promised Land. He is the victorious and noble king David bringing all rebellious power to subjection. He is the King who brings us into peace. He is the Prince of Peace! He is the magnificent and triumphant king Solomon governing his kingdom with peace and prosperity. He is the strong and powerful Samson who, by his death, has overwhelmed all enemies.

1 Corinthians 15 tells us that Jesus is the true and better Adam who passed the test in the garden and who gives us the reward of His obedience. It's as if *we* become obedient—although our obedience is frail and imperfect, Jesus imputes to us His perfect obedience. Jesus is the true and better Abraham who stepped out in faith to create a new people for God, and you and I are included in that family!

Whether you are seventeen years old and have recently been called into full-time ministry or you have been in ministry for decades, the goal of your life and leadership is not that people would esteem you but that they would esteem Christ—not that they would celebrate you, but that they would celebrate Christ—not that they would think you are amazing, but that they would think that Jesus is amazing. When you minister and lead, the goal is not that they would like you, but that they would love Him! This brings me to the ninth sign of sonship. A Christian leader who's going through the process of a leader enjoys empowering others for the glory of Jesus.

9) EMPOWERMENT—SONS EMPOWER OTHER SONS

One of the best ways you can communicate this to the church or the business you lead is to surround yourself with leaders who are more talented than you. Ask yourself, *Am I, without hesitation, willing to give talented leaders more authority? If not, why? Is there any sort of fear in my heart that they will be liked more than I am?* If so, rid yourself of that insecurity—today! Repent of it. Remember that Jesus is the hero of your church or organization, not you.

I remember being about six months into my role as a senior pastor; it was 2018. I went to a little diner in Cortland after church with a couple who visited that day. The woman kind of chuckled, saying that she didn't know who the pastor was for the first forty-five minutes of the service. She said someone opened the service with a welcome, and she thought he was the pastor. Then someone else lead worship, and she started to wonder if he was the pastor. Then, a young man closed the time of worship with a passionate plea, almost a mini devotional. She assumed he must be the pastor. Then a woman gave some announcements, and she said, "I wondered if *she* was actually the pastor!" She continued telling me, "It wasn't until you were about ten minutes into your sermon that I realized you must be the pastor!" I jokingly replied, "My goal is that everyone would find Jesus to be the center of our service. I feel one of the ways I do that is to include a team of leaders around me—people who discover their leadership potential. My goal is that Jesus would be so celebrated that I could be forgotten."

Pastors, my question for you is this: if you were to be in a tragic car accident today, could your church still function? If not, then too much is centered around you and your abilities. You must start to find a team of can-be-leaders that you can equip to do the work of the ministry. You can also start to staff people around you who are more talented, more anointed, and more able to preach Christ. In doing so, you will accomplish what John the Baptist had in mind in John 3:30 when he said, "I must decrease, and He must increase."

And if you're thinking, *I do not have the budget to bring on a staff*, then you are sorely mistaken. Vision requires no money. You can get alone with God and get vision with no money in the bank at all. All it takes to begin is desire. You can ask God in prayer, "Who has leadership potential? Who can I invest some time into and develop?"

Ask the Father for the eyes to see them, likely sitting in the pews in front of you every single Sunday. There are men and women with massive leadership potential—some of them with an anointing to lead and even preach. All it takes is that you ask the Spirit to open your eyes to see them. Once you begin to meet with them regularly to teach them what it means to follow Christ and to lead others, you will begin to make a greater impact for the kingdom. Not everyone belongs in your inner circle. Pray and choose wisely.

THREE, TWELVE, AND THE CROWD

Jesus had three closest to Him—three in an inner circle—Peter, James, and John. Jesus had twelve disciples who went almost everywhere with Him. They felt like spiritual sons to Jesus. Jesus also had crowds occasionally. I'm afraid that, today, many Christian leaders have crowds and no sons.

Love empowers. Loves gives the mic away. Love is generous with authority and blessing. Love doesn't hold on too tightly. Love doesn't manipulate or control. Love gives encouragement and empowerment. Love gives opportunity and second chances. Love dies to self and puts others ahead of itself. Love comes from sonship.

||||||||||||||||||||||||||||||||||||||||||||||||||||||||||||||||||||||||||||||||||||||||||||||||||||||||||||||||||||||||||||||||

You can love those you lead by giving them authority and blessing to reveal Christ to the nations! Jesus is the hero. Not me. Not you. Right now, this may seem like the Holy Spirit is bringing a loving discipline, but Scripture says, "That's a good sign! It's a sign of sonship!"

Consider Him who endured from sinners such hostility against Himself, so that you may not grow weary or fainthearted. In your struggle against sin you have not yet resisted to the point of shedding your blood. And have you forgotten the exhortation that addresses you as sons? "My son, do not regard lightly the discipline of the Lord, nor be weary when reproved by Him. For the Lord disciplines the one He loves, and chastises every son whom He receives."

It is for discipline that you have to endure. God is treating you as sons. For what son is there whom his father does not discipline? If you are left without discipline, in which all have participated, then you are illegitimate children and not sons. Besides this, we have had earthly fathers who disciplined us and we respected them. Shall we not much more be subject to the Father of spirits and live? For they disciplined us for a short time as it seemed best to them, but he disciplines us for our good, that we may share his holiness. For the moment all discipline seems painful rather than pleasant, but later it yields the peaceful fruit of righteousness to those who have been trained by it. —Hebrews 12:3–11

That passage reiterates this principle of sonship over and over, reminding us that, even when we are pruned, it is a sign of the Father's love for us. Throughout Scripture, God reveals Himself as Father, calling His people "My children." You only need to read a few chapters into the story of Exodus to hear God speak to His people as a loving Father.

This is how you must begin to see God. Before you lead people, you must allow God to lead you. You must allow His love to permeate your very skin and bones. You must understand who you are in light of who He is. He is *Abba*, Father. He is compassionate toward you and loves you unconditionally and unequivocally. He feels the same way about you as He does the prostitute who's selling her body this evening, or the drug lord who's been deceived into a world of crime. He loves them as much as He loves you. His love for man has nothing to do with man's performance. Before you can lead them, you should love them. Leading without loving will turn you into a tyrant. Leading while loving will reveal you as a servant.

10) COMPASSION

As the leaders of the church, we must realize that every person who walks into our building is either a *found* son or daughter of Father God or a lost child of God. He wants you to see every person for who they are! They are a potential child of God!

SONS SEE PEOPLE MORE THAN NUMBERS

This concept is also true if you're a leader in the marketplace. A CEO recently told me about how his real estate company provides finances for mission trips. He has funded eight trips so far and has a passion to do more! God keeps blessing his business, and he simply keeps giving his profits away! This is a leader who understands sonship. This is a leader who has embraced the purposes of God.

Remember why Jesus came to us? It's been said, "The Son of God came as the son of man to make the sons of men, sons of God." Jesus makes you and me His brothers and sisters, and we must be reminded of that as Christian leaders. This mission drives out all insecurity and reminds us of why we're doing what we're doing.

WHAT CHILDREN DO

I've got four girls, and they are the joy of my life. Selah is my oldest and my scrappy, athletic Sporty Spice as we like to call her. Elli, our second, is our Princess Elli. Eva is just a "handful," as people say when they're trying to be polite. She's goofy and tons of fun. Eden, at only three, is just so sweet. They are all so different, and yet I love them all equally. God feels the same way about you and me, and even that neighbor of yours who drives you crazy. Even the coworker who is always late to deliver. God loves every single human equally and that love simply won't change. He's Father.

I'm no parenting expert but . . . wait a minute, I hear you're deemed an expert when you've worked in a field for ten thousand hours. That means I AM an expert. Shoot, I'm a genius by that standard! Actually, if I'm honest, I'm like every parent out there—doing my best and hoping I'm not screwing things up. I have noticed some beautiful things in being a dad—some things I'm hoping can become takeaways for our understanding of how we can and should relate to our Father God.

CHILDREN KNOW THEY NEED HELP

Kids know they need help. Well, sometimes. If you're like me and parenting four girls, you know that they can change their mind in .0000002 seconds. One minute, I hear a panicked screech: "Dad! I can't get this shoe on! Why won't you help me!?" I bend down to help and hear, "Leave me alone! I can do it myself! Let me do it!"

Ugh! Confused. Again. This. Is. My. Whole. Life.

Really, there are plenty of times when my girls simply know they need help. Whether it's reaching something since I'm so tall or tying their shoes or homework. Children know they need help, and when they know they're loved, they know they can ask Dad for help.

Do you know you're loved? Do you know that you have a Father God in heaven who cares for you more than you could ever understand? Do you know that He is not only able to help you but also willing and desiring to help you if you would only ask? I want to say this again: God reveals Himself in many ways in His Word, none more prevalent than that of being our loving Father.

Simon Sinek, best-selling author and speaker, says, "Too many leaders worry about being in charge and forget their real job—that leadership is really about taking care of those in your charge. Leaders need empathy and perspective."[5]

You will have more empathy when you realize that your team members are humans just like you. They have fears, dreams, hopes, insecurities, prayer requests. . . . Your first job isn't to lead them over the hill; it's to care for them and ensure they know how loved they are by Father God.

---

5   Simon Sinek, *Best of Live2Lead*, 2016.

11) CURIOSITY

Children are naturally filled with curiosity and wonder. My kids, especially at that toddler age, would often ask, "What is that? Why are you doing that? Where are we going? What will happen if I eat this?"

One of the greatest attributes of a leader is curiosity. I know, you may not have expected that word, but the more you look into the leaders who've shaped our world and even our faith, they all were curious—curious as a three-year-old exploring their world, learning, seeing, touching, eating, and feeling something new every day. The greatest CEOs are curious about how the market will respond to a new product. They're curious about how their service or product could be better. They ask the right questions. They want to know why something works or doesn't work. They are curious about how to be better leaders and more inventive.

The greatest engineers and scientists are curious. Every inventor who ever walked the earth invented out of a seed of curiosity. Are you curious? Or are you stuck? You can't be both. If you're curious and if you love to learn, you and your organization won't be stuck for long. You'll be trying new things and honing in on what works and, before you know it, you'll be more effective than ever. Curiosity is the first step toward greater productivity, team unity, and successful leadership. If you feel the answer is "no" to that question, then I have to ask you to check for pride. Because humility leads to curiosity that leads to innovation and leadership. Pride leads to stagnation that leads to failed leadership and a team who knows it isn't valued and products or services that aren't wanted.

THE FATHER'S WORLD

When I take my kids to the sledding hill in our town, I give them all sorts of rules and instructions. "Put on your hats. Put on your snow pants, then your gloves, then your coat. The coat will help hold your gloves in place. Stop taking your sister's gloves!" The instructions continue. There are benefits that come with following the rules. For example, "You cannot get in the car until you have all your snow stuff ready. You don't have to walk there if you'll pay attention. You will not go sledding if you don't put that coat on. You will get hot chocolate if you guys stop arguing." Hey, no shame; bribes work, people.

I'd like to think that Father God goes on the adventure with us. When we are curious and set out in faith on a new adventure, God is with us all the way. I love going sledding down the hill with my girls, especially when it's a bit icy and we hit Mach 4. They take turns sitting on my lap, and we zoom down the hill screaming. I'll never forget a hill I took them to near Stony Glenn campground. We go there as a family for a getaway each winter, and while we were sledding down the huge hill nearby, a dad and I struck up a conversation. He asked, "Did you take them to the big hill yet?" I was like, "The big hill? There's a bigger hill than this?" He told me where to go and off we went.

Let's just say it wasn't the smartest dad move. It was twice as long and much steeper. They were a bit reluctant to go down, but I convinced them. Selah, my oldest, is adventurous and athletic, so she just went for it. She hit a sweet ramp about two-thirds down the hill and got some air. Eden was four at the time, and I told her I'd hold on and she'd "be fine." She climbed on and I aimed a little left of that ramp that Selah hit. Let's just say . . . there was another ramp. We were flying! About half way down this thing, I saw the ramp and couldn't adjust course. Everything went into slow-mo. I said, "Oh . . ." and up she went. I made good on my promise and grabbed her mid-air, but she came crashing down on me and we took a good tumble. There were some tears, but we made a memory! What's my point? I went with her! God your Father is with you in this thing!

Children learn that they live in their father's world—that someone else is in charge and setting the rules. They learn quickly that to disobey leads to punishment—or at the least, course correction. They learn that they are not the center of the universe. This lesson takes time, at least in the Biel household. They learn correct perspective. I'm afraid there are far too many Christian leaders in churches and companies who are hesitant to obey Father God's words. They are content to simply do what's "normal," because they're afraid of failure, man's opinions—or worse, change. But often, God's instructions to us require change.

Children even hold parents to their word and are ready to hold them accountable to even the principles they've established in the home. Children trust their father to hold true . . . well, most the time. One principle I've repeated in our home is sharing—the importance of being generous and giving away what is yours for others to enjoy. My toddler Eden held me to this standard a few months ago when I pulled through a drive through to get a coffee. Before I continue, you should know that my wife, being a nurse, calls any candy or treats "sugar." "No sugar before bed. . . ." "No sugar right now. . . ." "You have to eat dinner first. . . ." You get the idea.

So I paid for my coffee. I went to the next window and got it. Eden said, "What is that?" I said, "Coffee." She said "What's in it?" I said, "Coffee." It was early. I wasn't ready for a lengthy conversation, but she persisted: "What's in it?" I said, "Hazelnut, cream, and sugar." I happened to look in the rear-view mirror to catch her face when she replied with her eyebrows raised and a condescending tone: "You share your sugar!" I almost spit my coffee out everywhere. For the next ten minutes, I tried my best to communicate to her that I was unable to extract the sugar from the drink and share it with her. She was not cool with that and broke down in tears, insisting, "Shawa youwa shugaaa!" Another dad-fail for the books.

My kids inevitably trust me. When they feel in danger, they run to me. When they feel hungry, they come to me. They know I'll feed them (in due time). When they are hurt, they come to me for solace. They trust me. They really do. Why? It's simple. I'm their dad. Do you see God that way? If not, I encourage you to try to. Ask God the Father to reveal Himself to you in this way. Let God reveal Himself to you the way He did to Jesus: "This is my Son in whom I am well pleased." Let God reveal Himself to you the way He did to John, who repeatedly addresses God as a "Father" to be loved, trusted, and obeyed.

SONSHIP IS A PARADIGM

Leadership in the kingdom of God is about knowing that every person you lead is a child of God, whether they are living in Father's home or whether they are far from home and need to come home and be forgiven. You must care for them like the Father cares for them. Ask God to give you His heart for them.

What leadership is all about is caring for the people with whom God has entrusted you. It's not about having the highest position. It's about having compassion on those you lead.

It's not about having power. It's about empowering those you lead. It's not about being the smartest person in the room. It's about asking the right questions to evoke the best advice from the smartest people in the room—those you've put in the room because you know they're smart. A real leader doesn't take credit, they take responsibility.

God the Father, Holy Spirit, and Son are all three working in unity to create sons and daughters! He chose you to be a part of that! He knows what He's doing. He chose you and me to partner with Him! Remarkable! Because of this, we should be prayerful, courageous, humble, gracious, secure, grateful, focused on Jesus, empowering, compassionate, curious risk-takers!

APPLY IT

Group Discussion Guide | P.R.O.C.E.S.S. | Week 4

I'd like you to take a few minutes and circle the attributes you feel the Holy Spirit is speaking to your heart about in the list below. After you've circled at least three, take a few minutes to pray, ask the Holy Spirit to help you in these areas, and then write down what you'll commit to doing to grow in those areas. Make the commitment a commitment to God—a prayer. Share this commitment with a friend or your spouse. It makes the commitment more meaningful and more likely to be enacted, because you're inviting them to hold you accountable to it.

SIGNS OF SONSHIP

Circle at least three you need to grow in.

» Prayer life

» Courage to lead change

» Courage to confront

» Humility

» Graciousness

» Security (as opposed to insecurity—the need to prove your value)

» Gratefulness

» Christ-centered Speech (as opposed to "I" centered speech)

» Empowerment of Others

» Compassion

» Curiosity

» Risk-Taking

» Celebration of Other Leaders/Pastors (seeing them as brothers and sisters)

» Empathy

» Good Listening

» Belief in Father's Provision

My Commitment to Grow in Sonship

Lord, I commit to grow in sonship. Help me to see myself as a child of Yours *before* I am a _____ (your role at work). Remind me that, like Jesus, you have found pleasure *in me* before I ever perform anything *for* You. Remind me, Father, that when You see me, You see Jesus! In that, You are well pleased. Help me to be a good steward of the assignments You've given me in the season You've placed me in. Lord, I commit to grow in these areas by taking intentional time to do the following:

Celebrate the work of _____, a colleague of mine.

Ask my team good questions about their family life. I will take time every _____ to ask _____ questions such as, "How is your walk with God going personally?" "What are some victories and answered prayers in your life right now?" "What are some points of frustration or pain?" "How can I pray with you about those things?" "How can I support you in that? Is there anything I can do to help?"

Commit to my staff/team: I am here for you whatever you need. Truly, if you need to just talk, I'm here. If you need a day off to take your spouse out for your anniversary, take it! I want the best for you more than I want the best for this organization. I'm committed to your success!"

Take time every single morning at _____ to pray and read Your Word and invite Your Spirit to speak to my heart, challenge me to change anything in my life that needs to change to make me more like Your Son, Jesus.

Set aside time with a mentor and spiritual parent such as _____ at least once a month to come under their spiritual covering and receive wisdom. I commit to contact them today to start this relationship.

FINAL THOUGHTS

I hope you enjoyed this book and that it has encouraged you to press on to see the promise God's put in your heart come to life! In the next book, we'll look at the process of David, Nehemiah, and Daniel. I'm praying their stories inspire you like they inspire me.

While the *Process of a Leader* books are written for those in Christian leadership and ministry in their discovery of *why*, my book *Leverage Leadership* is written with the aim of answering the question of *how*? In it, I take you through the four essentials of every successful team. There are four things that every winning team has. Do you have them? While this book deals with the heart, *Leverage Leadership* will share more of the pragmatics of leadership and how to get from A to B.

I want to invite you to subscribe to my email newsletter in the footer of JordanBiel.com to ensure you're informed when that book is released. You can also click "Follow" on Amazon, and they will notify you any time I am releasing a new book. My prayer is that you'll love Jesus even more and be equipped to do the good work He's placed within your heart.

LETSLEADTHIS

LETSLEADTHIS is a network of Christian entrepreneurs and leaders who want to grow together, network, and build friendships. We have a Facebook page where you can get weekly motivation and advice on biblical leadership. We invite you to join us! If this book has impacted you and helped you as a leader, then know that it's just the tip of the iceberg of what you can learn from being a part of the LetsLeadThis network. Dr. Sam Chand, President Emeritus of Beulah Heights University, says in his masterclass, "Many leaders know where they want to go, but haven't packed their bags yet. They have a vision for where they want to go but haven't packed their bags with preparation for the journey." LetsLeadThis is part of packing your bags and getting prepared for the journey ahead. Learn from leaders and entrepreneurs who've gone before you, so you can go further and stay healthy in your journey. Learn more at www.LetsLeadThis.com.

To get consistent motivation, practical leadership advice, and biblical inspiration on leadership, follow our page on Facebook @LetsLeadThis or find my podcast by searching "Jordan Biel" on Apple Podcasts, Spotify, or anywhere you stream.

Remember, you believe in God. It's time you realize that He believes in you! There's a promise in you! There's a prophetic picture of your future! Rise up in faith and start taking steps in that direction! Visit TheProcessOfALeader.com to view videos that are perfect for a mentoring group. There, I will summarize the chapter, include a few new aspects of Joseph's story, Gideon's story, etc. I'll also ask some questions for you and your team to discuss. The videos are free and I truly hope they bless you and that you are filled with the joy of sonship!

Discover Jordan's Worship Music

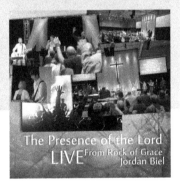

Scan the code to visit Jordan on Spotify

9 781954 089952